only one sky to fly in

embracing the reptiles

Jacqueline Maria Longstaff

First published in November 2000 by Singing Heart Publications
www.singingheart.dk

Second edition published in May 2003 by TSG –
Hidden Mysteries, Texas, USA

Third edition published in September 2003 by Quester Publications.

 **Quester Publications**
PO Box 3226
Chester
CH4 7ZB
ENGLAND

Copyright © 2000 Jacqueline Maria Longstaff

No part of this book may be reproduced in any form
without permission from the Publisher, except for the quotation
of brief passages in criticism

Cover photograph:
"Entering Denmark Through A Summer Sky"
taken by Jacqueline

Design and production by Samantha Masters
Printed and bound by Intype Libra Ltd, London

British Library Cataloguing-in Publication Data – a catalogue record
for this book is available from the British Library

ISBN 0-9541904-4-0

Dedication

To The Inner Guru – the deepest potential in each of us.

Thank you

To Jacob Norkov Friis, Denmark – for your help and friendship.

To Jill in New Zealand for your help.

To the energy I call 'The Ruby Red Reptile' – thank you for helping out when we needed you.

To John Wragg from Sheffield for looking after me.

To those I have met and talked with around the world who have also provided me with pieces for this jigsaw puzzle: David, Gillian, Donald, Jörgen, Gary, Narcis, Jeremy, Beverley, Storm and many more.

To Alan Ploug and Lotte Fyhn from Denmark for helping me to the top of Arunachala on the final day of the 20th century and for helping me down again on the first day of the 21st. I recently heard Kirsty MacColl singing a song on the radio. She sang, 'In these shoes – no way José!' I remembered the climb up and down Arunachala!

Many thanks to Mark Hopkins in Wales for proof reading and to Cynthia Kasireddy in Santa Cruz, California for the use of her computer whilst preparing the second edition of this book. A big thank you to Jocelyn Savage and Hidden Mysteries for taking on the second edition and to Sam Masters in England for her layout and design for the first and third editions.

Finally, thank you to Neil Hague and Quester for publishing the third edition.

Other publications by Jacqueline

In English

Books   ***The Last Waltz** – me and my shadow collectively speaking*
Singing Heart Publications
Orders: www.questerpublications.com

***Knock Knock – Who's There?** More than an autobiography*
Singing Heart Publications
Orders: ashramsingingheart@yahoo.com

***Only One Sky To Fly In** – Embracing the reptiles* (2nd edition)
TGS Services 22241 Pinedale, Frankston, Texas 75763, USA
Tel 903-876-3256
USA and internet orders: www.hiddenmysteries.com

Video   *Who Are The 144,000 Sundance Teachers?*

More information about Jacqueline's work and Singing Heart can be obtained from:	**John Wragg** **10 Beaufort Road** **Sheffield** **S10 2ST** **England**

In Danish

Many 2-hour radio programs produced by Jacqueline can be obtained from:	**Radio Lotus** **Nannasgade 20 st.** **2200 Copenhagen N.** **Denmark**
More information about Jacqueline's work in Scandinavia can be obtained from:	**Suchata** **Stenlillevej 17** **2700 Bronshoj** **Denmark**

The woman with the stars in her hair

Sketch by Amanda Slack –
reproduced here with many thanks

After being given a copy of this sketch
and reconnecting with my life as Nada in Sirian Egypt
circa 10,700BCE, the following words came…

I feel you playing through me – Oh gentle star of Sirius
I feel you in the heat of the golden Sun
I feel your liquid light vibrations
Your joy and creativity in perfection

Many incarnations will pass before we meet again
    in this land
The time will come on far away shores when the
    connection is renewed
I will recognise you, my sacred cosmic lover
And we will fly together beyond the bounds of Earth
And bring new realms, new joy, new light
To those who've long forgotten the glory deep within

Together we reactivate the codes
Together we will teach them how to fly
In the distant future which is already now
A cosmic celebration of Sirian Sun and light.

          Jacqueline Maria Longstaff
               May 2000

Contents

Preface to the third edition 1

1. *Introduction* 3
2. *This vast emptiness* 10
3. *Please don't mention David Icke or the conspiracy* 16
4. *Who are the reptiles?* 24
5. *The challenge of the reptiles* 53
6. *Shape-shifting* 83
7. *Visions in the jungle* 99
8. *The missionary position – reptilian style* 117
9. *Embraced by a reptile* 138
10. *Royal Command Performance* 145
11. *A guiding hand from Sirius* 172
12. *Bill and Ben the Flowerpot Men (leading humanity up the garden path)* 187
13. *Shamballah – inner state or inner Earth?* 200
14. *Has the contact begun?* 222
15. *Arunachala* 229

Index 235

Preface to the third edition

I am happy to present the third edition of *Only One Sky To Fly In*. To be really honest, my heart was not in the first edition. I wrote it because I was asked to and somewhere it felt right to do so, but I didn't really want to get into the reptilian story! However in the two years that passed since the first edition was published, I received much more information and had insights that I felt were worth sharing in a second edition published in the US. Now comes the third edition.

When asked if I "believe" in reptiles I never give a yes or no answer. There are many levels from which we can approach the topic and I do hope this is obvious from what I write in this book. I am aware of the fact that the whole subject is wide open to manipulation because of the fear it instills in many people. Finally I am also aware that the information connected with this subject will not necessarily take people to the space I believe is the next step for most on their spiritual pathway. However I hope there are sections of this book which do nourish this next step.

So here is the book. I hope you will find answers to some of your questions and inspiration for some of your next steps.

Jacqueline Maria Longstaff (June 2003)

I

Introduction

I have known for some time that I have to write this book and actually started to write it under the title "Only One Sky to Fly in – The Final Surrender". The focus of the book was to be higher consciousness. However as the first pages started to unfold I could feel that for some reason I had to let go of my original idea for the presentation of this subject and instead write a short account of my perspective on the reptilian story. I had expected just to include this story in a book about higher consciousness. Those who have read my first book, "The Last Waltz", know that I describe it as "the enlightened consciousness embracing the collective shadow". During one of my trips to Findhorn in Scotland where I have often presented some of my work, a man came to me and said, "Jacqueline, you attempt to bring together some very interesting polarities!"

For me there is nothing strange in bringing together subjects such as enlightenment and the conspiracy or higher consciousness and the reptilian agenda. I know this has resulted in some people not being able to understand my deeper message – especially people who want lots and lots of facts about the conspiracy to satisfy the mind. Others, who understand and love my deeper work, have not always been able to accept my involvement in the subject of the conspiracy.

Another incident comes to mind as I write. Some years ago in Denmark, I was talking to a friend, an English man, who is well known in spiritual and astrological circles. I told him David Icke would soon be joining me again in Copenhagen where he'd be giving an evening talk and then we'd hold a weekend event together. I asked my friend if he'd be interested in coming to the talk. He said he'd try to come and added, "So, you're involved with David Icke are you? Oh well, you've always been out on the fringe haven't you darling?"

I was amazed, as it seems I'd imagined all those I was connected with were out on the fringe! I was truly amazed to realise this was not so – to realise that the fringe had a fringe and that I was on it! Today I can see that those of us who go into the areas touched upon in this book have really left the shore of respectability far behind. Barbara Marciniak uses the expression "systems busters" and it fits well. However let us be aware that in order to really be a systems buster it is first necessary to bust one's own system and break free of conditioning. If this is not done one is still plugged into the system one claims to be busting and the term "systems buster" is just another cliché. We systems busters usually have a strong Uranian aspect in our astrological charts or horoscopes. Uranus is "the awakener" – the "systems buster" and as I have an Aquarian ascendant it rules my chart. A few lines from Thoreau sum up the Uranian archetype perfectly:

> "If a man does not keep pace with his companions
> Perhaps it is because he hears a distant drummer.
> Let him step to the music he hears
> However measured or far away."

There are some of us who seem to hear the drummer with whom the distant drummer keeps pace.

As you read this book please be aware that I do not write it to add to the drama and sensation which already surrounds the subject of the reptiles and I do not pretend to be an "expert" on this topic. I know there are many who have done years more research than I have. I write it simply because I have been asked to and feel it is right to do so. Much has been written recently about the reptiles – a subject many find distressing. I hope that some of what I have to say will help to give a balanced perspective and remove some of the fears and misunderstandings that have arisen amongst people.

There are many angles from which to view this subject. I simply tell the story of how I heard about the reptiles, the experiences I have had and the information I have been given to pass on in this book. There is much more information available and suggestions as to where to obtain further information are given throughout the book.

I also presume readers have some knowledge of spirituality and higher consciousness and do not intend to go through the basics. You can read about my own spiritual journey in my second book, a kind of autobiography, entitled "Knock, Knock – Who's There?"

With regards to the manipulation of consciousness on the planet (popularly called "the conspiracy") I also presume the reader has basic knowledge in this area. My first book, *The Last Waltz*, gives a general introduction to this subject as do many books and magazines available today. If you want the basics but don't want to be bogged down by thousands of pages of research, try David Icke's *I am me I am free*. For the more adventurous try an older book of David Icke, *...And The Truth Shall Set You Free*.

Perhaps I should also say here that there are different terms used for those who play major parts in manipulating and controlling events on this planet. Those used most often are the Illuminati and the Brotherhood. I have used both terms in this book.

I would also like to say something I stated clearly in *The Last Waltz*: I do not judge any part of the drama, which is playing itself out here on this planet. I feel there are issues we need to look at and embrace as we journey through this great lift in consciousness we have incarnated to participate in. I see only one movement of life – one consciousness expressing itself in many costumes on many stages. I see millions of dramas being played out simultaneously and in this "eternal now" there do seem to be pasts, presents and futures depending on how you view the reality. There is also much suffering on this planet – suffering which feels very real for those who experience it. The fact that the reptilian story is coming to the surface is, for me, a sign that it may soon be possible to move to a level of consciousness where much of this suffering will disappear.

In my second book, I told the story of inter-dimensional contacts I had in the late seventies and early eighties and feel it is appropriate to repeat this story here.

The first significant event happened in India in 1979. Fully awake, I was "sucked" out of the top of my head and found myself flying through the cosmos. A voice said, "We have been waiting for you." When I returned to my physical body I was in a heightened state of consciousness and lay awake all night in a state of bliss. After this episode there were many similar spontaneous happenings. I did nothing to provoke such things and as I have written many times before I kept my focus on the deep inner process which was unfolding. I had chosen the path of Self-Realisation and was wary of psychic phenomena and spectacular experiences, which could divert me from this pathway.

In 1980 back in my apartment in Copenhagen, I was sitting on the bed one evening and felt the energy in the room intensify to such a pitch that I seemed to hear it buzzing. I then became totally paralysed. Next to the dining table in front of me two very beautiful beings began to manifest – one quite tall and the other smaller. They looked as if they were made of lustrous multicoloured gemstones and the love energy emanating from them was enormous. They did not attempt to communicate with me through speech but just seemed to watch as my seven main chakras[1] began to spin violently and my whole energy body was activated. I was already well-trained in meditation and was able to witness the whole happening without fear. I actually felt totally safe and have no idea of how long I was paralyzed or how long these beings were with me. At some point I could begin to move my physical body again and the beings slowly demanifested.

Similar things happened in the days that followed. Suddenly I would experience the very high-energy field, the paralysis and the activation of the chakras and energy bodies. However I did not see the two beings again. One thing I noticed was that I suddenly seemed to understand many things without knowing how I understood them. It was as if I had had an extra lift in consciousness and the vibratory rate of my energy field accelerated to such an

---

[1] Chakra is a Sanskrit word meaning wheel. Chakras are wheels of energy which rotate in the etheric body or aura connecting us with different aspects of reality. For example, the heart chakra connects us with experiences of unconditional love, acceptance and compassion.

extent that I often found it difficult to lie still in bed at night. In time I seemed to get used to this new state.

Shortly after this event, and without my mentioning it, I was told by a well known Danish psychic that he had to inform me I'd been contacted by higher space intelligence and prepared for the work I was to do at a much later date. Some years later I was also to learn that I came from the Andromeda Galaxy.

The following information may also be of interest. I've seen artists' depictions of what people claim to have seen during similar contacts. However, up until early 1999, I'd never seen anything which remotely depicted what I saw that evening in Copenhagen. Then in 1999 I went to have a look at a newly opened museum in Blackpool, England – The Alien and UFO Exhibition. There was a section that reminded me a little of a wax museum. In it were life size figures of interdimensional beings in glass cases and when you pressed a button the case lit up. I found it quite amusing, but was amazed when I pressed the button for the seventh dimensional being. It looked so similar to what I saw all those years ago. Shortly afterwards I was re-reading Barbara Hand Clow's book, *The Pleiadian Agenda* and came across her description of the seventh dimension:

> "seventh dimension – lines of communication for pure thought. For Earth, the seventh dimension is the galactic information highways of light, the photon bands, that are guided by the Andromeda Galaxy".

So perhaps this is enough of my old story – enough to establish my "credentials" for writing such a book! I hope you enjoy this book and that it provides some light and nourishment. It is simply another brick in this great cosmic jigsaw puzzle so many of us are helping to put together at this moment in 3rd dimensional time.

2

This vast emptiness

"The moment you sense that painful feeling within you say to yourself, "I love this feeling. I welcome it. It doesn't have to go anywhere or change. I accept this feeling." And the warmth which is always there, moves over to this "rock" and begins to smooth it, surround it, and make it porous. So out of the power of your love for this "rock", "it" takes on the power of your love. It becomes filled with your love! Love pours through this "unlovely" feeling-mass, surrounds it, uplifts it, and it becomes "lovely". And you find you are capable of holding two things: your love and that agony. Your love is so vast that there is nothing that it will not hold, and using that vastness is what you've got to learn. No grief is so great that you cannot hold it within you and also hold the vast power of your love at the same time. You do not have to choose. You can have all the grief, you can have all the illness, you can have all the sorrow, all the regrets, all the guilt, and there is no need to worry because all the love in your heart is so vast it will hold anything."

"I Come As A Brother" – Bartholomew

This passage from "I Come As A Brother" is actually a passage I have often read to people during events I have held. It is so simple and yet it reveals the deepest mystery of the heart and contains a most important message for seekers of enlightenment: everything is as it is. However if you cannot embrace what is, if you resist the flow of life within you and lose contact with your heart, then suffering arises. If you resist the inner flow of life you cannot embrace the outer. I often say that if you cannot embrace yourself, you cannot embrace the universe. I also say that whatever applies individually also applies collectively and as people individually learn to accept and embrace the individual shadow, humanity collectively prepares to accept and embrace the collective shadow. This shadow includes the reptiles.

I remember that many years ago, a spiritual teacher I knew named Michael Barnett expressed something similar to the Bartholomew text above using different words. He said that once people had had a taste of enlightenment it was as if they then had to learn to hold on to enlightenment with one hand and work on their "stuff" with the other hand. Enlightenment doesn't go anywhere, but people often close down and turn their back on this space when they meet painful situations or inner states. The most direct way in to this space is through the heart. It lies deep within, through the layers of the heart chakra. It is a vast empty sky – a vast emptiness – which reveals to us the secrets of consciousness itself.

I remember a song we used to sing at the Osho ashram in India where I stayed for a few years in the late seventies:

> "There is only one sky to fly in – only one sky
> There is only one sky to die in – only one sky."

This sky in which the so-called "ego" dies and we then fly free, is this vast inner emptiness. In it, everything one thinks one is – all false identities – simply dissolve and the creative flow of life or God is experienced. In this sky the pain and the joy, the light and the dark are not weighed or judged. They are simply recognised as experiences emerging from and dissolving back into the divine play of consciousness. This emptiness is neutral, fearless and is one with everything in its nothingness. It is not really possible to describe it in words, although certain words do seem to come close and when we reach this state we tend to use similar words to describe it. I also call this state the Inner Guru. What is the Guru? It is a principle and the deepest potential within each of us. "Gu Ru" means the dispeller of darkness or the destroyer of ignorance – ignorance being a mistaken idea that we are separate from the whole. People are attracted to the outer Guru for different reasons, but often because of the unconditional love and acceptance emanating from the Guru or Self-Realised spiritual teacher. This love and acceptance comes from the direct realisation of the inner vastness. When this state becomes one's reality an outer teacher or guide is no longer needed. When each individual reaches this inner vastness each reaches the same sky – there is only one. In this sky each individual shadow is dissolved and freedom arises. It is also in this sky that the reptilian drama will finally be embraced. Until that time there is still much to be done as the collective hand grasping planetary enlightenment grows stronger and the other hand works on the collective "stuff".

    I would like to share with you a couple of things, which may also help to give a taste of this inner sky. The first is a simple exercise, which was actually created by Michael Barnett. He used to call it "The 3 Levels Exercise", and it went something like this:

Sit comfortably with closed eyes and place your hands on your knees, palms down. Now take a look at what may be called ordinary reality: the palms of your hands resting on your knees. Next you will be asked a simple question which can be answered on three levels. The question is: "What is happening here?"

The first level answer is, "The palms of my hands are resting on my knees". Easy! And if other people came in and were asked what was happening they'd be able to agree that this was what was happening. It would be a shared reality.

The second level reality has to do with existential realities. Bring your full attention to your palms resting on your knees and ask yourself how it feels. Describe the sensation. If you are asked from this level what is happening, you may reply "I feel pressure on my knees" or "I experience a warm, tingling sensation." This is your experience in the moment – your individual reality. You are connected to your own energy system and twenty other people sitting in a similar position could have twenty different experiences of reality on this level. All would be valid.

Now let's move to the third level. The question for this level is: What is happening where your palms meet your knees if you don't put words on the experience – don't call it anything? You can't "answer" the question if you are not to call it anything, but this experience may give you a taste of this inner vastness. It seems that on the third level we have a common experience, just as on the first level. However it is not a consensus reality of the mind, but a communion of something much deeper. It is a shared reality – a transcendent reality far beyond the mind.

To be one with this reality you must first allow yourself to taste the level above – the level that can be labelled. Here you experience the hope, fear, anger, excitement, jealousy or whatever appears. When you can feel comfortable doing this you can then experience these movements of life and still stay in touch with the third level. Then, with time, this third level which cannot be described, reveals the vast emptiness – your true nature.

I'd also like to share a few lines from an old text by Sengtsan: "hsin hsin ming". This text describes The Great Way – the Path as it is often called – the Path to Enlightenment.

"If you wish to see the truth
then hold no opinions for or against anything.
To set up what you like against what you dislike
Is the disease of the mind."

Later on in the text it says:

"Do not search for the truth;
only cease to cherish opinions."

Opinions have to go – there is no place for them in this inner sky. This is just the way it is and to argue for or against this is simply the mind thinking it knows. I'm just giving a different kind of hint here – different things work for different types of people. This vast inner sky seems to insist that certain things be left behind at the entrance. At the opening to the deeper levels of the heart, labelling, judgement, and opinions – all tools of the mind – have no place.

This inner space where all can be embraced is your home and the goal of your deepest longing. Whenever you feel there is a part of you that is still difficult to accept, close your eyes and go as deep into your heart as you can. Take this aspect of yourself with you. Don't try to sort it out or make it improve in any way. Just be there with it allowing the Inner Guru, your deepest potential, to take you beyond the whole drama.

You may wonder what this chapter has to do with the subject of the reptiles. I include it for several reasons: First of all this was to be the way I would have started the book "Only One Sky to Fly in – The Final Surrender", a book about higher consciousness. This is always the essence of my teaching no matter which umbrella it is presented under.

Secondly, I see that reaching the level of consciousness described here is now the next step for thousands of people here at the beginning of this new millennium. A decade from now it will probably be the next step for thousands more.

And finally, it may serve as a reminder that it is this level of consciousness many of us have incarnated to hold or "anchor" here on Planet Earth in order that humanity may pass through the revelation of the agenda of manipulation as smoothly as possible.

So, let's move on now to my part of the reptilian story.

3

Please don't mention David Icke or the conspiracy

When David Icke sent me a copy of the first draft of his book, *The Biggest Secret*, I had to laugh at the title he'd chosen for chapter two: "Don't mention the reptiles". As he wrote in the book some people had urged him to write the basic story of what is happening on the planet – including the murder of Princess Diana – but had warned him not to mention the reptiles. David Icke, being who he is, told the full story from his perspective. After receiving the book I told him that no one had, as yet, told me not to mention the reptiles. Instead I was often told that people would love me to come and share my energy and work with them, but "please don't mention David Icke or the conspiracy".

I don't want to comment much on this as I said pretty much what I needed to say about this attitude in *The Last Waltz*. All I'd like to say right now is that perhaps we could all just try to trust the flow as we play out the parts we are here to play. I remember a very fine psychic I once talked with who tuned in to some of the work David and I were doing together at that point in time. She talked about those of us who were really working for peace and who were willing to offer everything for it. She said that before we could achieve this peace we are working so hard for, a lot of very peaceful people would have to make a lot of trouble.

So to those who have difficulty accepting the script some of us seem to be following please understand that some incarnate to "make waves" and that there are many different types of pieces to fit into this great cosmic jigsaw puzzle. I would like to acknowledge David Icke here for his commitment to truth and his courage to do it his way. I don't agree with the whole of David's interpretation of the reptilian story or accept every piece of information he has received, but I do feel he holds a very large piece of the puzzle. For me, a quotation he often uses describes him perfectly:

> "Today's mighty Oak is just yesterday's nut that held its ground"!

There are many, myself included, who believe David Icke was set up with some misinformation in order to discredit him. If this proves to be true let us be aware that this probably happened because David has come so close to uncovering the truth of what is happening on this planet. For example, his book, *The Biggest Secret*, contains very valuable research into the murder of Princess Diana. On the subject of the reptiles this book also contains serious information about activities at Denver Airport and Dulce Base in New Mexico. What can be done about the thousands of human beings, many of them children, who are being held as slaves in reptilian bases? In *The Biggest Secret*, chapter 16, we read about babies who are born and bred in captivity simply to be used as human sacrifice. Whether David was set up or not, I'd say he needs our continued support and not condemnation.

When I was first introduced to facts about the manipulation of consciousness on the planet there were three things I learned from David Icke which stood out for me as being especially important. One was to help people understand that the "demonisation" of true spiritual development, presenting it as dangerous, crazy, "occult and therefore to be avoided" etc. was actually a powerful tool used to rob people of the very thing which would set them free. Real spirituality lifts people to a level beyond the low vibrational energies on which this agenda works. The second important point I felt was for people to understand that whenever they turn against each other and promote separation – because of race, religion, educational status or whatever – they give away so much power and continue to feed the illusion of separatism and duality. Finally, a very important message: whatever happens *don't* get microchipped!

For more information on microchipping I recommend a short, easy to read booklet written by Nick Sandberg,[1] entitled "Blue print for a Prison Planet (The Plan to Microchip Humanity… and why you won't believe it)". I feel that almost everyone should read this booklet! It's also a good one to pass on to the staff of your local bank. It is almost impossible to obtain a Visa card today that doesn't have a microchip in it.

Remember, we can talk about enlightenment and planetary initiation but if people are microchipped there will probably be no enlightenment for them. Each individual microchip can be traced and your consciousness can simply be shut down if you are a threat to the elite agenda. This is perhaps the main reason I still feel it is necessary to speak and write about such things.

---

[1] Published by: Relax UK Ltd, D'arbley St, London W1V 3FG. Contact the author by email at: nicks22@onetel.com

Travelling on the Caltrain during a recent visit to California I saw an advert in the newspaper for a "Vaccination and Microchipping Clinic" in Novato. I asked a fellow passenger if people actually had microchips inserted under the skin at such clinics. He assured me they did and added that it was a wonderful way to ensure you could find your child again if he or she went missing. He then told me that there had been a big campaign to find missing children in the US and as part of that campaign the photos of missing children had been put on milk cartons. As a result many people had now decided to "get their children done"! This was exactly what David Icke predicted some years ago. I remember him telling me about the milk carton idea in the US. He said it was being used to attract attention to the missing children situation and that the "solution" which would be offered was microchipping.

I was in England in September 2002 just around the time of the murders of two young girls, Holly Wells and Jessica Chapman. It was a high profile case with a very sad outcome. I had the feeling that this case was going to be used to promote the idea of microchipping children and, sure enough, that was what happened. Just a couple of days after the bodies of the girls were discovered, about an hour of a popular radio show was devoted to the subject of microchipping. A twelve year old girl and her mother were interviewed – both seemed very happy that the girl was to be microchipped. Apparently you can get a chip in the United Kingdom for only twenty pounds.

I have been informed that very soon it will be time to put into practice something else that will be a major step along the road to microchipping. It is the introduction of the "Smartcard" – the beginning of the cashless society. Every kind of information including our bank details, medical records and employment records will be put onto one card. Once this system is in place it will not be long before there is some "problem" with cards being lost, stolen or ineffective and the next step will be the microchip. There are plans to introduce the Smartcard in many cities in the world.

Early in 2003 my webmaster gave me a copy of a statement he had taken from the internet in connection with IDC's Telecom 2003 conference that was to be held in Denmark 9–10 April. The statement said that British futurist Ian Pearson, who would be in Denmark for the conference, predicted that everyone would have a microchip operated under the skin. He predicted this would happen sooner than people imagined. In his booklet Nick Sandberg has a chapter entitled "The Future – Chips with Everything?" I say we already know that too many chips are not good for us – so let's say no before it's too late!

Even though I write this book which focuses to a large extent on the extraterrestrial question, I'd like to say that I'm also wary of some of the information being put out about extraterrestrial manipulation of consciousness. I am especially concerned that the sensationalism of such information may divert people's focus from areas we still need to focus on. We still need to be awake as to what is happening in the banking system and the economy, and to be aware of microchipping, mind control techniques and the misuse of advanced technologies. One book I recommend on the subject of mind control is the late Jim Keith's book, *Mass Control – Engineering Human Consciousness*. It does not surprise me that shortly after publishing the book he became the late Jim Keith!

We also need to be aware that certain things that are happening to people can be blamed on extraterrestrials and thus take our attention away from what some of the governments are up to! In an interesting book: *Encounter in the Pleiades: An inside look at UFOs,*[2] I found a similar theme in the following passage from the chapter entitled "Star Wars":

> "Genetic programming suggests something far beyond the prospect of biological warfare. It includes the possibility of scrambling or rearranging our DNA. This type of thinking is prevalent in certain New Age dogma, which indicates that the human race is currently undergoing a transdimensional change. Angels or the like will appear and rearrange your light body so that you resonate with a higher octave. This may be true but it is much more theoretical and other worldly if angels and other dimensional beings are doing it. If the secret government or the military industrial complex has this capability, we are dealing with an undeniable real world scenario."

Perhaps I could also say here that archetypal energies being projected into our Solar System can be grasped and interpreted on both high and low vibrational levels. In this way similar themes can be played out simultaneously on many levels and I'd say we need to be willing to look at all levels in order to see what's what. Astrology actually describes for us the play of archetypes I refer to here.

Before the second edition of *Only One Sky To Fly In* was written David Icke wrote another book, *Children of the Matrix*. This book contains a great deal of information on the reptilian agenda (and much more) and I do recommend it. I'd like to quote a passage from the book describing the very powerful force controlling the planet today:

---

[2] Preston B. Nichols and Peter Moon. (Sky Books – New York)

"New Agers and others talk about the need to balance male and female and they are right. But we lose the plot if we don't understand that there are different levels of this fusion. You can fuse the negative aspects of both energies to create a malevolent "third force" or you can balance the higher frequencies of male and female, so creating a positive third force. The world around us is, in fact, the manifestation of the negative balance and interaction of these energies."

Many people today talk about the importance of bringing back the feminine energy. However David goes on to explain that, even though many believe we live in a male-dominated world, it is actually the negative expression of the female energy, which controls from behind the scenes. We see the negative expression of the masculine energy out there in the world. It is easy to see the military power and aggression and the control exercised by the bankers and multinationals, but they are actually put into power by a hidden force. He says they are put there through covert manipulation and that the Illuminati are dominated by the negative female energy. I would say that we could also look at this symbolically. The masculine and feminine energies in most human beings are not in balance and this is reflected in the world we have created.

Those who have been following the unfoldment of the reptilian story may know that David Icke has been criticised by Ivan Fraser of *Truth Campaign*.[3] I have read what Ivan has written about the reptilians and other aspects of the conspiracy. I also feel he holds a piece of the puzzle and appreciate many of the articles he has written. I would also say that it's important that we all share the information and

---
[3] A UK magazine

insights we have – we are all working towards the same goal, aren't we? So I did find it strange that Ivan Fraser presented his criticism of David's research together with attacks on his personality and gossip about his private life. I felt it was strange to do this at a time when it is so important we all support each other. So many conspiracy researchers, Ivan included, talk about the "divide and rule" technique used to keep humanity at each other's throats and therefore out of balance emotionally and spiritually. I have had some communication with Ivan and know he wants to heal this situation. I hope it is possible to do so.

Something I feel is very important as the collective shadow comes to the surface, is to focus on ways of releasing the inner dignity at the core of each human being – the potential to be all that one may be and not to settle for less. I read an article in a newspaper about George Orwell's *1984* "predictions". The journalist said that many things Orwell wrote about have come true, but that there seemed to be one thing he didn't take into account.

> "He underestimated the power of the human spirit."

It is the human spirit, which will guide us through the times ahead. I see the human spirit as that part of a person, which is always connected – connected to an energy not caught up in the drama being played out. I see it as the part which, even though it may seem to experience a feeling of fear or limitation, is always beyond this experience. I know there are many of us now who help to nourish this aspect in others because we have found it within ourselves.

4

 *Who are the reptiles?*

On the evening of the 30th May 1993 I was doing some ironing at home in the center I had for ten years in Copenhagen, when something made me turn on the radio. The radio station I was tuned in to was Radio Lotus – a well-known spiritual radio for which I worked for several years. A young man I knew nothing about was being interviewed. His name was Jacob Norkov Friis and he was 26 years old at the time. Listening to him, I felt I knew him on a very deep level and made a few notes of what he was saying. The subject, space intelligence and inter-planetary co-operation, was not new to me – as I mentioned in the introduction to this book, I had already had inter dimensional or "space" contacts. I had also made a radio program and given other talks on the subject and knew that much more information would come to the surface as we reached the end of the century. However, I believe this was the first time I had heard anyone mention the reptiles. Here is just a little of what Jacob said that evening. I have translated from Danish.

We all live in different frequencies and it's possible to tune in to many levels of one frequency. He said that he came from the planet Kapella in Andromeda (i.e. Kapella was where he individuated) but that originally we all come from the universe's Central Sun. We have light bodies everywhere. In the age we are moving towards we will lift our vibrations and become one with that power which created us – the universal breath.

What is very important now is respect for and acceptance of everyone and everything created. This is what love is. There are brotherhoods on all levels. The reptiles belong to a lower frequency and represent an absence of light. Everyone must learn love – do not judge. It is love, which protects us.

I was aware of a very powerful love vibration and great wisdom and authority coming from him, and actually imagined he was much older than 26 years. Next morning I phoned him and invited him to come to Singing Heart Center. He said he could feel he was meant to do some work at the center and we arranged to meet. That was the beginning of our friendship and also of much work we have done together on the radio and in other ways. We actually made about 20 two-hour radio programs together and they proved to be extremely popular.

Jacob has some very remarkable gifts, which I sometimes describe as "being born without the veils going down." He can see clearly into and travel in all dimensions of consciousness. His clairvoyant readings give a very clear understanding of this present incarnation because of his ability to see past experiences of life in light bodies on all of these dimensions. His gifts have also been valuable for me in my research into the manipulation of consciousness and the extraterrestrial themes that link into this.

I should just like to make a couple of things clear here so as not to be misunderstood. First, I am not a "conspiracy researcher". As I wrote in the introduction to this book, my work is first and foremost concerned with higher consciousness – Self-Realization, and yet this path forced me, and many others like me, to question why the real search for higher consciousness has been so rare on this planet. This of course takes us into the area of the manipulation of consciousness.

Secondly, I'd like to say that I have been quite wary of channels, clairvoyants and psychics. There are some very good ones, but many more that I do not feel support a real path to enlightenment although they have their place in the greater scheme of things. However life does seem to have provided me with two people with very exceptional gifts. Jacob is one of them. The other, who lives on the other side of the world, knew nothing about my work when I met her and knew very little about what was happening on the planet. She seems to have similar gifts to Jacob and during the interviews we've had together she has also been able to provide me with much valuable information. Very often, without her knowing it, she has confirmed research done by myself and others. She's very down to earth, practical, naturally spiritual and a real healer. She didn't want to get involved in "all this stuff", but it seems life persuaded her to! I agreed not to use her name throughout the book, but will get her messages across in one way or another.

During one of the first talks Jacob held at the center I remember him saying something which made much more sense to me some years later. He said that because the vibrations on the planet are rising as fast as they are people would soon be able to see into other frequencies and would therefore have to be able to live side by side with the reptiles. For some reason what he said stuck with me. I had no idea at the time that I'd one day be writing a book about the reptiles. However, if we look symbolically at what Jacob said, let us also remember what happens individually as people open up to more light. As we open up to light the shadow is seen more clearly. It is the same collectively. People often ask me if I believe there are real physical reptiles or if I feel they simply represent a particular state of consciousness. I would say that both possibilities seem realistic to me.

In the mid 1990s I read a couple of Barbara Marciniak's books and especially felt very comfortable with her book entitled *Bringers of the Dawn* which contains much information about the reptiles and the reptilian agenda in connection with Planet Earth. Before we look closer at this agenda perhaps I ought to give some basic information about the reptiles for those readers who are new to the subject.

"The reptiles" is the popular name given to an extraterrestrial race or genetic stream that is said to have been controlling Earth and humanity for thousands of years. It is said that, in one form or another, their genetic bloodlines are manipulated into positions of power and have infiltrated every structure on this planet – political, religious, military, media, economic etc. They use lower vibrational energies such as fear, guilt and aggression to manipulate consciousness. This is done by orchestrating wars and famines, stirring up racial hatred, denying people an enlightened education, filling them with unhealthy food and dangerous medicines, keeping them busy and entertained so there's not time to ask too many questions about the nature of life and so on. Just as some of us seem to have an "agenda" or natural inclination to lift the consciousness on the planet, the reptilian force seems to have the opposite agenda. Their agenda seems to be to prevent this from happening and to keep the planet imprisoned in this low vibrational energy on which the reptilian consciousness feeds.

In his fascinating book, *Blue Blood, True Blood*, Stewart Swerdlow says that although the Reptiles were the first to colonise Earth there were also 12 other groups who donated DNA to the experiment. He says the result was "a general free-for-all". When I look at the wars and conflict on the planet today I actually see different groups of extraterrestrial origin fighting it out on the Earth plane.

I would like to quote a couple of passages from a book entitled *The Active Side of Infinity*, written by Carlos Castaneda. I believe it is the last of the Castaneda books and was published in 1998 by Harper Perennial. The following quotations are taken from the chapter entitled "Mud Shadows" where don Juan talks about the flyers' mind. He claims it is the predators who have given the flyers' mind to humanity. I would suggest we could read "reptilian consciousness" for "predators".

> "What I'm saying is that what we have against us is not a simple predator. It is very smart, and organized. It follows a methodical system to render us useless. Man, the magical being that he is destined to be, is no longer magical. He's an average piece of meat. There are no more dreams for man but the dreams of an animal who is being raised to become a piece of meat: trite, conventional, imbecilic."

> "Sourcerers believe that the predators have given us our systems of beliefs, our ideas of good and evil, our social mores. They are the ones who set up our hopes and expectations and dreams of success or failure. They have given

us covetousness, greed, and cowardice. It is the predators who make us complacent, routinary, and egomaniacal."

Where do the reptiles come from? There are several answers to this question depending upon which level we are focussing. We could say that originally, like everything else in creation, they come from the Creative Source – also called God. Jacob would perhaps use the term the Central Sun. We could also say they are simply aspects of us on a low frequency and reflect to us humans our shadow. We attract this reflection because, collectively, we are not dealing with the issues the reptilians confront us with – especially the issue of claiming our own power. More about this later. On another level we could say that as long as this planet is in a state of duality there will always be some who play the good guys and some the bad guys.

We could also try to answer the question from a historical perspective by looking at some of the research done in this area. This is what I shall do now and there are suggestions at the end of this chapter if you would like to read more about the ancient history of the Earth.

In *Children of the Matrix*, chapter 6, David Icke takes us back hundreds of thousands of years to Lemuria and Atlantis and says that there was widespread extraterrestrial and interdimensional activity on Earth during these times. He says that many Earth races were seeded during these times and writes about the battles which went on in different parts of the galaxy. David especially mentions battles between a blond-haired, blue-eyed race known as "Nordics" from Lyra, the Pleiades and Aldebaran and factions of a reptilian race from Draco, Orion and within the Sirius network. Regarding these battles David Icke says:

"This battle on Earth is symbolised by stories such as the Phoenician "St. George" defeating the dragon and "St. Patrick" removing the snakes from Ireland. But there was also crossbreeding between the serpent race and the Nordics, which created the hybrid bloodlines that overwhelmingly became the ruling bloodlines of the Aryan dynasties."

On the reptoid website (**www.reptoids.com**) there is an excerpt from John Rhodes' book *Dragons of the Apocalypse* which says:

"There is more than enough evidence to indicate that a highly evolved reptilian life form is interacting with human beings. Their presence has been witnessed in every corner of the Earth by people from all walks of life. Now that we have established the fact that they are here, the next question to address is: Where are they coming from?"

He goes on to say that the evidence suggests there are three different theories as to the origins of reptilian life and that there is a large amount of data supporting each theory. I feel that all three are possible simultaneously. They are:

1 **Extra terrestrial** – from another planet or star system,
2 **Inner terrestrial** – residing in the inner Earth
3 **Inner dimensional** – existing in other vibrational levels than the third dimension.

Some research suggests that some reptiles come from the Draco constellation. This system includes Thurban, which was at one time the North Star point of orientation for the

Pyramids of Egypt. It seems several ancient monuments are aligned to this constellation and it is interesting to see that a sketch of the outline of the constellation of Draco does actually resemble a lizard!

Many people today are aware of the books of Zecharia Sitchin and I do recommend his latest, *The Lost Book of Enki*. Sitchin is an expert in ancient languages, including Sumerian, and has translated the ancient Sumerian clay tablets, which tell the story of the Anunnaki, an extraterrestrial race that first landed on Earth some 450,000 years ago. They are said to come from Nibiru, a planet in our solar system, which orbits our Sun every 3,600 years. It seems Nibiru is actually an artificial planet created by the Pleiadians and was used to seek out raw materials in our solar system. The Sitchin translation of the Sumerian Tablets say that long ago Nibiru almost destroyed a planet between Mars and Jupiter – a planet the Sumerians called Tiamat. The Tablets say the Asteroid Belt was created by a collision between Tiamat and one of Nibiru's moons, and it is also said that a part of Tiamat eventually became Earth. Sitchin's studies show that the Sumerian culture was established by Nibiru, sometimes called "the planet of the crossing", and that its 3,600 year elliptical orbit takes it between Mars and Jupiter and then far out into space. Scientists have located something beyond Pluto and called it Planet X and there are actually people who speculate that when this Planet X again passes close by Earth it will bring the return of the Anunnaki. There are discrepancies in translations and other kinds of research but this is the general idea, and there are many indications of something either existing or passing between Mars and Jupiter, which is of significance to our planet.

As I updated the second edition of this book there was much speculation in certain circles about the exact time of the return of Nibiru and the Anunnaki. There were many who predicted the return in 2003 and there is a whole website dedicated to stories about this and the devastation it will bring to planet Earth. I do not feel that 2003 is the correct date. I cannot see any astrological evidence to suggest it is so. In June 2002, together with a research companion, I had several meetings with Credo Mutwa in South Africa. Credo is one of the last remaining Zulu shamans and the official historian of the Zulu nation. He is a very wise man with an amazing amount of knowledge. We talked about Nibiru and the Anunnaki and he said that although Nibiru may be sighted in 2003 the date for its return is about 2015 – 2018. You can read more about Credo Mutwa throughout this book.

I also talked with a well-respected white South African psychic who told me that an extraterrestrial group working for planet Earth had an assignment to prevent the return of Nibiru causing the catastrophes which normally accompany its return. Apparently the disturbance caused to Earth's magnetic fields as the planet passes close by is what causes the accompanying earthquakes, tidal waves and possible pole shifts. There have also been reports recently in the mainstream media about an asteroid coming close to Earth's orbit and some say this is in fact Nibiru. Initially the date given for the passage of this asteroid was 2003 but that was later changed to sometime after 2010. If Nibiru is artificially engineered that may explain why it is being described as an asteroid and not a planet. It also makes sense to me that something can be done to alter its course and prevent these catastrophes from happening. I would also suggest that the level of consciousness we are able to reach collectively before Nibiru's return will also greatly effect what happens.

I recently received a copy of an interesting email. It refers to Enki, an Anunnaki god, who you can read about a little further on. I include the main message of the email here:

> "Funny how NASA launched contour yesterday with the intent on studying two comets. The first in 2003 just happens to be named "Encke". If that doesn't ring a bell to some see Sitchin's new book, *The Lost Book of Enki*. Who is Enki you ask? The lord Enki is an Anunnaki god who tells the story of extraterrestrials arrival on earth from none other than Nibiru".

I have actually been told that the Anunnaki come from many parts of the galaxy, but have a kind of head quarters on Nibiru. The Sumarian texts say that they created Homo Sapiens by genetic manipulation to help them mine gold. Apparently there was a crisis on Nibiru caused by the use of nuclear weapons and a special kind of gold was needed to build an atmospheric shield. The texts state that the first Homo Sapiens were created from the genes of the Anunnaki together with the genes of ape-like creatures who hung from the trees in Southern Africa. This would definitely explain the "missing link" enigma. Many attempts were made before the right kind of genetic structure was created and it is written that Anunnaki females carried the embryos in their wombs until the time came for the birth. The brilliant Anunnaki genetic scientist who was responsible for the success of this project was subsequently given rulership of the earth. His name was Enki.

On page 100 of Sitchin's book, *The Lost Book of Enki*, we read:

> "Where to obtain gold from Earth's bowels he then determined.
> What heroes to the task are needed he calculated, what tools were required he contemplated:
> An earth Splitter with cleverness Enki designed, on Nibiru that it be fashioned he requested,
> Therewith in the Earth to make a gash, its innards reach by way of tunnels:
> That-Which-Crunches and That-Which-Crushes he also designed, on Nibiru for the Abzu to be fashioned."

The "Abzu" refers to Enki's gold-mining domain in Southeast Africa. I found it interesting that Credo Mutwa told us there is a very special gold found only in South Africa. He said this was the gold mined by the ETs. There is far more gold in Eldorado, South America and other places, but they chose Africa. He said the oldest mines in the world are found in South Africa and Swaziland and researchers had found two types of mines. There were the later ones that had been mined by black people but there were older, deeper mines where the rock had been cut with very strange technology. Apparently the rock there had been sliced like bread.

Another interesting source of ancient Earth history is a book written in the form of a novel entitled "Inanna Returns". The Earth is referred to as "Terra" and this is what is said about her inhabitants during the early visits from Nibiru:

> "Enki and Enlil, the two sons of Anu, had been assigned to bring gold and other useful minerals back to Nibiru. Gold was essential to us because of the imbalances in our atmosphere brought about by our incessant warring. Terra in those days was seen solely as a source of minerals, a mining outpost at

the edge of the galaxy. Its inhabitants were the wild creatures who roamed her vast plains grazing on an abundance of grasses, and the races of the Snake People and Dragon People who preferred to live in the vast tunnels under Terra's crust to protect themselves from the frequent radiation storms and magnetic shifts."

The author, V.S. Ferguson, has drawn heavily on Sitchin's research and I found it very entertaining reading. I also felt it gave a true picture of what happened all those years ago and clear suggestions about what we can do in the time ahead.

There are scientists today who support Sitchin's view of history. Not so long ago when the American Voyager space probes photographed the recently "discovered" planets Uranus and Neptune, scientists were amazed to see that Voyager's description of these two planets fitted those given in the Sumerian texts thousands of years earlier. These texts support similar versions of the history of Earth given by many indigenous peoples including the Aborigines, Hopi, Mayans and Tibetans.

According to Sumerian texts Enki, the son of an extraterrestrial king, was a benevolent ruler. However, humans were seen as beasts of burden and treated cruelly by other groups of extraterrestrials including Enki's brother Enlil. Apparently Enki tried to stand up for the humans and he is said to have created the "Brotherhood of the Snake" to fight against the enslavement of humanity. The Brotherhood was concerned with spreading spiritual knowledge and with the attainment of spiritual freedom. The snake was a much-revered animal and throughout time has also been worshipped as a symbol for the consciousness and sacredness of nature. Today many of us still associate it with the awakening and raising of the Kundalini energy and with subsequent spiritual enlightenment.

However the Brotherhood of the Snake failed to free humanity and modern research shows that the organization was eventually taken over by the controlling force on the planet – sometimes called the "Illuminati" – and used as a tool to suppress consciousness. In *Children of the Matrix* David Icke says,

> "The reptilian bloodlines covertly operating within the human society created many of the ancient Mystery schools to hoard the knowledge of true history, and the esoteric and technological expertise of Atlantis, Lemuria, and the post-cataclysmic world, especially the Sumer Empire. They also ceased control of the other Mystery schools, which were formed with a more enlightened agenda. This was one of the roles assigned to the Royal Court of the Dragon (also known as The Brotherhood of the Snake) from around 2000BC when it infiltrated the more positive Egyptian Mystery schools and made them vehicles for the reptilian "gods".

It also seems that a certain group of malevolent extraterrestrials have never lost control of Earth and can manifest here physically and astrally in different forms, including reptilian form. This however is not the only form, and I feel it is important to remember this as I see a very negative thought form being built up around reptiles at this moment in time. A reliable contact who has begun to see this malevolent group in manifestation describes those she has seen as "a kind of cross between a snake and a dog". Others see different forms and the ability to shape-shift is also acknowledged.

It is believed by some that the Anunnaki are a reptilian race and that they are the same race who are referred to in the Bible as the Nephilim.[1] At one point in his latest book, *Genesis of the Grail Kings,* Sir Laurence Gardner is discussing where the Anunnaki and Nephilim come from:

> "In this particular instance, I can find absolutely no way to explain the phenomena of the Anunnaki beyond that which was originally recorded – and text after text says precisely the same thing: they were the 'mighty ones of eternity', the 'lofty ones from on high', the 'heroes of yore'; their Nephilim ambassadors 'came down' and their 'kingship' was lowered from heaven".
>
> "Quite what these beings looked like is impossible to say, but the numerous Sumerian portrayals of the gods and goddesses are generally quite human in appearance. There are, however, some archaic figurines from around 5000BC which depict them with expressly serpentine features."

Gardner also states that the community of the Nephilim gods are sometimes referred to as the Elohim – a name used for them in the Canaanite and Hebrew traditions. He says, however, that going back further in time to ancient Sumer the name for the "Divine Lofty Ones" was Anunnaki meaning "Heaven come to Earth". He tells us that the Grand Assembly of the Anunnaki met at the Temple of Nippur and that this court was a prototype of the one attended by Jehovah of the Old Testament as described in Psalm 82.[2]

---

[1] In Hebrew this translates as "gods who came down to Earth"

[2] "God presides in the heavenly council; in the assembly of the gods he gives his decisions" New Life Good News Bible – Harper Collins

According to ancient texts the Anunnaki later interbred with their creation and thus created a crossbreed elite. Investigative research today suggests that this elite outwardly rules our world and yet, even though they may seem to be in positions of great power, they are simply puppets overshadowed by their other dimensional rulers. Some researchers even say that some of today's rulers and leaders are actually full-blooded reptilians hidden in human form. (This gives a whole new meaning to the song, "I've got you under my skin"!) This hidden force constantly manipulates the minds and emotions of human beings thereby trapping them in a low level of consciousness – a third dimensional drama which is simply a manifestation of lower fourth dimension (or lower astral) energies. Hence the fear, guilt, aggression, competition, experience of separation and the suffering which for thousands of years has more or less been accepted as life on planet Earth.

When I look at information from the Sumarian texts and other sources, it seems that one of the most important figures behind the manipulation we are still faced with today was Marduk. He came from Nibiru. He was the firstborn son of Enki who was later worshipped in Egypt as Ra. He was said to be jealous of his brothers and from his city, Babylon, he claimed supremacy on Earth. I get the feeling that Marduk is the energy behind Jehovah of the Old Testament. In her novel, *Inanna Returns*, V.S. Ferguson writes:

> "As long as the human beings believed that they were powerless, they could be entrained to worship Marduk in all his disguises. Always looking outside of themselves for help and comfort, the human species remained weak and vulnerable to Marduk's ingenious enslavements."

When I was first beginning to learn about the hidden manipulation on the planet I was surprised to find out how much satanic ritual, including human and animal sacrifice, was going on in the world. (Remember the Old Testament is full of such sacrifices!) Later I understood that the energy created during these rituals actually links the participants to the lower fourth dimensional energies and reinforces the connection to this negative stream of consciousness they serve. The rush of adrenaline when the victim is sacrificed pulls in the reptilian vibration to such an extent that there are reports of reptilians manifesting here in the third dimension and of shapeshifting. Although I feel there is truth in some of these claims I also feel that there is some misinformation and perhaps also misinterpretation of certain reported happenings. I go into more detail about this in a later chapter.

With regards to the reptilian race I'd suggest that they and other species have manipulated consciousness on this planet for a very long time. Although I don't agree with everything in Virginia Essene and Sheldon Nidle's book, *You Are Becoming a Galactic Human,* I do feel a lot of the information on Earth's "forgotten history" makes interesting reading. The book goes back 35 million years to a time before there was physical life on this planet and tells about an etheric life form which was created to act as a kind of guardian species for our solar system. This life form was to look after Earth until a few million years later when a physical life form developed which could replace the etheric life form. Apparently the creative plan for Earth was for it to be an experiment in diversity – many different life forms developing side by side and sharing guardianship of Planet Earth.

We are also told that about 26 million years ago two non-human groups arrived and began to establish colonies. One was a reptilian group from less well-known stars in the constellation Sagittarius, and the other was a dinosaurian group from the Bellatrix system of Orion. (I find it interesting that, at this point in time when so much information is coming to the surface about the reptilians, the planet Pluto is moving through Sagittarius. Pluto is the planet of transformation – of death and rebirth. It brings to the surface that which is hidden in order that it may be revealed and transformed.) These two groups, seeing the whole galaxy as theirs to rule, also claimed Earth as their own. The etheric guardians and the angelic forces allowed this to happen with a view to changing the attitude of these two groups with the energy of love. For over 8 million years love energy was sent to them and they began to allow mammalian creatures to evolve. These creatures were the ancestors of today's dolphins and whales.

I also find this information very interesting, even though we have no concrete proof at the moment that it is true, because according to esoteric astrology and the esoteric science of the 7 rays, Earth is ruled by the 4th ray, which is the energy of Harmony through Conflict. This could certainly be seen to be the energy guiding this decision to allow such potential conflict and to attempt to bring it into harmony through love. The Solar System itself is said to be of the 2nd ray, which is the energy of Love-Wisdom. We often hear that "love is the law" and that, ultimately, "there is only love".

You Are Becoming a Galactic Human states that the three different civilizations developed well side by side, reaching a level of co-operation that was quite unique. About 10 million year ago a group arrived from Bellatrix and other stars in Orion and decided that such a system of co-operation did not fit with their vision of reality in which they saw themselves as rulers of the entire Galaxy. They planned to destroy the mammalian society. This resulted in the destruction of about 98 percent of the reptoid/dinoid society by the spiritual hierarchy of Earth, and the surviving two percent fled. They fled to a planet often referred to as Maldek, which is found between Mars and Jupiter. For millions of years there were other wars and take over attempts by the reptoid and dinoid civilizations as humans developed and built up colonies on Mars, Venus and Earth, but finally Maldek was destroyed and about 900,000 years ago Earth was again controlled by humans. This allowed Lemuria to rise and flourish until the Atlanteans destroyed it, aided by certain renegade groups from other star systems. It is said that the Atlanteans also developed a feeling of separation – of wanting to rule and be special. It seems this is the energy that brings the conflict – when the oneness is forgotten. Yet let us remember that this is also a creative expression of life, played out against the background of the one sky in which the whole of existence flies.

In *The Biggest Secret* chapter 2, David Icke also mentions the fact that there is still a connection between Orion and groups who are interfering with humans on our planet. He writes:

> "Beings from Orion and the Pleiades are among many other races reported by abductees and researchers to be interacting with humans. From what I hear from Brotherhood insiders who have seen some of these extraterrestrials, the Orions (a cruel, but beautiful race according to my contacts) have some kind of alliance with the reptilians."

Just one final point I'd like to make about Orion. It seems there were other groups from this system who were very advanced and very spiritual and I understand most of them were etheric in form. Orion is linked with the eighth dimension – a very high dimensional energy which "houses" the Galactic Federation.[3] The group from Orion who have brought so much destruction have done so through identification with a deep rooted idea about being special and thus having the right to dominate others. I remember Jacob and I talking one day about a mutual friend and Jacob said that this man's next step was to let go of his attachment to his Orion family. He said it was this particular energy that was holding him back, that he was not co-operating with those he was connected with and always wanted to be "number one".

Another aspect of this story that is also important to be aware of is that of the hierarchy within the reptilian ranks. As you will see when I introduce the Ruby Red Reptile in chapter 4, it seems there are groups of reptilians that are more advanced than other groups and also groups who are rejected by more highly developed reptilians. On re-reading this passage I remember notes I made from an interview I had with someone at the beginning of 1998. This person, who is able to see what is happening on many levels, suddenly asked me:

> "Does it make sense to you that there are "aliens" down here fighting other "aliens"?"

---

[3] My understanding of the Galactic Federation is that it comprises all energies working for the upliftment of consciousness throughout the galaxy. In *Blue Blood, True Blood*, Stewart Swerdlow writes that the Galactic Federation was initially formed by the Lyraens against Reptilian attack.

I replied that this was my understanding of what can happen. Then I was told:

> "There are heaps of people who are programmed and when I see them on TV I can see who is and who isn't. I've known for some time there was something strange about many people but I didn't know what it was. With regards to Sai Baba,[4] I used to think he was just a fad, but he's a strange one – really strange. He's another type of alien than Tony Blair. Blair is stronger than Sai Baba. Sai Baba has different powers but up against Tony Blair he'd be the loser."

I remember Jacob saying recently that different groups of ETs fight each other down here on Earth and that one of the techniques they use is to reveal negative things about rival groups and individuals. I have looked at this seriously with regards to writing about these things as, ultimately, such facts as I present in a book such as this are perhaps not going to take people beyond this drama and into the deepest level of themselves. I am aware of this each time I write about these things and yet I still feel it is relevant to write about such subjects.

In two videos, together entitled *The Reptilian Agenda*, David Icke interviews Credo Mutwa, the well-respected Zulu shaman from South Africa I introduced earlier. I really do recommend these videos in which Credo Mutwa shares knowledge which has been kept secret for hundreds of years. He tells the story of the "Chitauri" – the Zulu name for a reptilian race he claims has manipulated and controlled the world for thousands of years. He also reveals information about how the black magicians of the Illuminati

---
[4] A well known Indian Guru. Read more about him in chapter 5

use their occult knowledge in order to carry out this control. Credo Mutwa believes he himself was abducted and experimented upon by the Chitauri many years ago and tells the story during the video interview. When I spoke with Credo Mutwa he too said that different groups of ETs had always been fighting each other here on Earth and added that the Anunnaki were not so evolved spiritually. I experienced him as a very fine man who also holds some important pieces of the jigsaw puzzle.

Jacob also watched the videos in Denmark and could tune straight in to Credo. He felt that he was very sound and that his information could be trusted. One thing he said, however, was that people should know that the group of reptilians Credo refered to was not the same group who have infiltrated the governments and royal families. The latter are a more advanced group who actually, to use Jacob's words, "don't give a shit about the ones Credo Mutwa talks about". Those refered to on the two videos mentioned here belong to a pretty low vibratory level and I feel it is important to remember this. Many people find the whole reptilian subject very frightening and disempowering, and it is important to remember that we have the power and the awareness needed to overcome this perceived threat. We have the potential to lift our vibrations above the level from which these energies operate.

When something is hidden or in another dimension enormous power can be projected onto it – both positive and negative. This reminds me a little of people who project all of their own wisdom and spirituality onto some disincarnate entity contacted through "channeling". Now, some people are simply projecting their fears and phobias onto the reptiles instead of working through these fears. However, as

Jacob also pointed out, it is fine that Credo Mutwa has spoken up because it also helps to give credibility to David Icke's research. As I said earlier I don't agree with every bit of information David has put out, but his work in this area needs to be taken seriously. The fact that the reptilian story is so "way out" has resulted in some people imagining he has "gone over the edge" and they do not, therefore, acknowledge the rest of his work.

One of my sources, who wishes to remain anonymous, told me of some pretty "way out" information she received from someone who writes for one of the most prestigious scientific magazines in the US. This person told my contact that the governments know that the following story is true. I don't know whether it's true or not but share it here just for fun. I find it quite a fascinating theory! So let's go way back in time to when the reptilians and human based creatures first came to Earth.

Apparently the humans slept at night because they knew that this was when the reptiles came out and they were afraid of them. They would get up just before dawn and eat the eggs of the reptiles. The reptilian overlords saw the humans eating the reptilian young and found this repugnant. They therefore came down to Earth and, using DNA, changed the humans to pigs and ate them. The humans saw what the reptiles were doing and made a truce with them. They said they would not eat the eggs of the reptiles if the reptiles didn't eat them. I was told that this is why the idea of eggs and bacon for breakfast is coded so deep in the human psyche! I find it interesting that humans and pigs can actually exchange bodily parts.

Some time ago I received a card from a well-known and well-respected man whom I don't actually want to name here. He's old, deeply spiritual and he also worked in some capacity for many years with the United Nations. We often write to each other and I asked him if he had anything to say about the reptilian agenda. This is part of his reply:

> "A friend of mine in, I think, the Rockefeller domain, caught a glimpse of a conversation with a reptilian. They're not necessarily bad. A friend, travelling with a well-known space-interested person, was shown by him his actual reptilian nature. So they seem to be playing different roles."

I do feel it is important that we remember this and, as I said earlier, not contribute to the creation of a fearful, negative thought-form around all things reptilian. This will only contribute to the fear and negativity which keeps so much of the consciousness on this planet locked into the lower astral planes.

I mentioned earlier about reptilians being aspects of us and that they are in some way reflecting humanity's collective shadow. Much has been written about the area of the human brain called the reptile brain. A prehistoric segment sometimes called the R-complex drives this ancient part of the brain. According to neuroanatomist, Paul Maclean, this segment plays a big role in the following types of behavior: aggression, territoriality, the establishment of social hierarchies and ritualistic behavior. These are exactly the qualities displayed by those who are known to be at the heart of the manipulation of this planet. I have also been told that it is possible to isolate and stimulate the reptilian part of the brain so that its characteristics are over exaggerated. It is said that this is being done in different ways and partly accounts for the increased violence and aggression we see in the world today. This is one good reason for being aware of what one opens ones energy fields to through television, computer games, music etc. It can be useful to constantly check if certain experiences leave us feeling uplifted or drained. Do they bring more clarity, openness and harmony, or do they result in a feeling of disorientation, agitation or a feeling of being "speedy"?

I know of parents in Denmark who are very sensitive and who have expressed concern over various cartoon series the children watch on television. They can just feel that some of them produce disturbing reactions in the children and at the same time don't want to watch the children all of the time or dictate what they can and cannot do. I know this is a dilemma for many parents and appreciate the creative ways they try to find to tackle such challenges. One thing that seems to work, especially with older children, is truth – talking truthfully with them about such things and encouraging them to be aware and take responsibility for themselves in this area.

I was talking to someone named Susan in Denmark recently and she reminded me of the Healing-Massage Teacher Trainings I held long ago in Copenhagen. These were eighteen-month long training groups and people who took this training usually went very deep into themselves. I always said to them that they could not take other people further than they were willing to go themselves. The training program was divided up into four sections and in each section we worked with a different area of the body – physically, psychologically and spiritually. The massage itself was simply a tool that facilitated deep personal and spiritual development.

Susan reminded me how very different the four parts of the training were. As I looked back I remembered how much pain and resistance could come up in people during the first part when we worked on the legs and feet – the whole area connected with being on a physical planet. People often felt the urge to run away from the whole process. When we moved on to work with the lower torso and solar plexus area much anger would be released. The first couple of days could be quite challenging as people often started projecting all sorts of things onto each other and onto me and sometimes they didn't seem to get along together at all. I often had to ask the group to bring carpet beaters in order to release the built up aggression – release it onto a mattress or cushion of course! People were often surprised to discover what they held down in the "basement" of their being – often hidden behind a polite or sociable exterior.

The day Susan and I were talking together was actually the day after the very sad affair at the Danish Roskilde music festival where 8 young people were trampled to death. Susan said that she was grateful she had been to the depths of herself in the massage training because she now knew what she contained. She knew the power of her anger, the depths of her rage and knew that if she was pushed and trampled on she could probably react very strongly. I mention this because I feel it is so important that people consciously face their inner states, acknowledge them and learn how to use the energy constructively instead of being used by it. People who are afraid to feel their feelings and embrace themselves are far easier to manipulate as they are often willing to compromise themselves in order to escape feeling that which they wish to avoid.

When we moved on to the heart area in the next part of the training everything usually looked very different. There would be so much love, joy and creativity flowing that people met on a level where the "problems" which arose during the second section no longer mattered! When we reached the final part that focussed on the head, face, the upper chakras and higher consciousness we again had a completely different energy field. It would be more neutral and meditative. The love was still there but it was "cooler" and people were more detached. I remembered these times and realized how easy it is to stimulate certain states in people if one understands how to do this. I'm sure that much esoteric knowledge is being used to provoke certain reactions and states of being in people on this planet – states which further the negative agenda.

Someone who'd spoken with a man who used to work in the Israeli military also told me about the way soldiers were trained. She said they were trained to hold their weapons so the sexual organs were stimulated when the weapons were fired. They would actually get an erection and perhaps ejaculate. What a clever way to make killing someone fun! I'm pretty sure what I write here is nothing compared to what is being done in the military and other areas to ensure that people play the parts designed for them.

I'd say that each one of us has, or has had, the possibility of expressing R-complex qualities, and until humanity collectively moves beyond this level life will always reflect this back to us in some way. David Icke expressed the same idea on his website. He commented on the fact that the reptilian brain powerfully influences human behavior and that it is secretive and deceptive because it is hidden from us. He then went on to say:

"And this subconscious "secrecy" manifests physically as the Illuminati secrecy which has been unfolding an agenda for thousands of years while the people have remained oblivious of its existence. But because we are in the closing years of the current energy cycle, our subconscious is becoming conscious. As it does so, its physical expression (the Illuminati agenda) also becomes conscious and that is one key reason why the agenda is now being exposed for the first time on this scale."

(Taken from: **www.davidicke.com/icke/articles2/reptbrain.html**)

Something else which will be reflected back to us until we "get it right" will be humanity's great ability to give its power and authority to someone else expecting someone else "out there" to sort things out. Interestingly David Icke often likens humanity to a flock of sheep – the "baa baa mentality" – head down following the one in front! In esoteric astrology the sign of Cancer is referred to as the sign of the masses or the flock. The opposite sign, Capricorn, is the sign of initiation symbolized by the mountain goat climbing the mountain alone. (I am talking here of course about the soul's progression through the symbolism of the astrological signs. I do not mean that all Cancerians are of a "baa baa mentality"! Each individual horoscope is made up of many archetypes.) So as we approach the possibility of planetary initiation we will collectively need to demonstrate our ability to be individuals in touch with our own authority. Self-Realization is what is being offered – we are being challenged to find "the god within". As long as we don't do this, as long as people wish to worship someone or something outside of themselves, life will reflect this state of consciousness back to us. We will create a drama which includes some god to be worshipped and some authority to be obeyed. In her fine book, *Bringers of the Dawn*, Barbara Marciniak writes:

> "Wanting to have something to worship is the frequency control on Earth. What the planet is headed for is someone or something new to worship. That is the potential holographic insert – a new god to worship. The creator gods, the reptiles, know that their plan has run short, so to speak, and there is an intention of creating a new plan, a new diversion, a new disempowerment. Therefore, beyond anything else, listen to yourselves."

So we are approaching a great possibility on this planet as we approach a time where people will no longer look up to the skies – or the pulpits – for their "God" or the gods. People will listen to and trust the god within. As I see it we have the possibility of individual sovereignty and of releasing the highest creative potential in each human being. How smooth or how bumpy the ride before we reach this new level depends on us – on how quickly enough people wake up and take control of their destiny.

Suggested Reading –
Research into Earth and Extraterrestrial History

- William Bramley: *Gods of Eden* (Avon Books, New York).
- Barbara Hand Clow: *The Pleiadian Agenda* (Bear and Co.)
- Virginia Essene and Sheldon Nidle: *You Are Becoming a Galactic Human* (Santa Clara, CA: S.E.E. Publishing 1994)
- V.S. Ferguson: *Inanna Returns* (Thel Dar Publishing Co. Seattle, Washington 1995)
- Ivan Fraser: *The Truth Campaign* – numbers: 14, 15 and 16 (49 Trevor Terrace, North Shields, NE30 2DF, England)
- Laurence Gardner: *Genesis of the Grail Kings* (Bantam Press)
- David Icke: *The Biggest Secret* and *Children of the Matrix* (Bridge of Love).
- Barbara Marciniak: *Bringers of the Dawn – Teachings from the Pleiadians* (Santa Fe: Bear and Co.)
- Credo Mutwa: *Song of the Stars* (Station Hill Openings)
- Zechariah Sitchin: *12th Planet* (Avon Books, New York). *The Lost Book of Enki – Memoirs and prophecies of an Extraterrestrial God* (Bear and Co.)
- Stewart Swerdlow: *Blue Blood, True Blood* (Expansions Publishing Co., PO Box 12, St Joseph, MI 49085, USA)
- Robert Temple: *The Sirius Mystery* (New York: St. Martin's Press 1976)

Reptile website: www.reptoids.com

Videos: *The Reptilian Agenda (Parts 1 and 2)* – David Icke interviews Credo Mutwa.

Contact Bridge of Love Publications:
PO Box 43, Ryde, Isle of Wight PO33 2YL, England
email: dicke75150@aol.com

5

The challenge of the reptiles

These past few years Jacob and I have spent much time together in Copenhagen looking at the reptilian story. Not so long ago I remember him saying that one thing which is difficult when it comes to bringing up the subject of the reptiles is that it's almost impossible to find people who don't react strongly and close down in some way. I have also found this to be true. I can understand why people said to David Icke "for God's sake don't mention the reptiles!" Yet perhaps we should also remember that Earth is a planet where many types of beings come to develop free will, and therefore the reptiles have just as much right to be here as any other group. There are many frequencies within the different dimensions but our physical senses only seem to be tuned to the frequency we operate in on an every day level, and therefore many presume that we are all there is to "intelligent life" on planet Earth. It is a bit like believing there are only certain colors in our color spectrum and, because we cannot see it with our physical eyes, not realizing that there exists, for example, infra red.

However it is important to remember that this is a planet where we come to experience the development and use of free will. Any group who acts against the free will of human beings is not acting in accordance with the rules of the game here and for this there are consequences – consequences, not judgement. This also applies for those working for the so-called "light". Always we seem to come back to the importance of non-identification with the role being played!

In this chapter I have, amongst other things, another type of reptile story to tell – something that began back in October of 1998. Hopefully this story will help to balance some of the "horror" stories many have heard about the reptiles, but first I shall have to provide some other rather unpleasant details so you can understand the conversation Jacob and I were having.

We were sitting in a café in the center of Copenhagen, enjoying cream cakes and cappuccino and as usual discussing what was happening on the planet. We were talking about the fact that there are many who have reported seeing politicians and other well known figures whose names come up again and again in conspiracy research, change into reptiles. There are many accounts of people witnessing politicians and members of the Royal Family taking part in satanic rituals, which include human sacrifice. Here are a couple of examples.

In the summer of 1996 I accompanied David Icke when he went to the north of England to interview a woman who was actually born in Darlington – the town where I myself was born and went to school before becoming a Danish citizen. We went to see the woman concerned because she wanted to speak out about her childhood experiences in satanic rituals in the Darlington area and her story was horrific. She was probably the most traumatized woman I had ever met. Amongst other things she told how she was brutally raped many times by Edward Heath. After the interview David dropped me off in Darlington where I was spending a few days with my mother. Later that evening I switched on the television news just as Edward Heath came on – apparently celebrating his eightieth birthday! He was laughing – the same laugh the woman had described earlier that day. This may not be significant, but life often gives me simple little confirmations of things which I need to be aware of for one reason or another. You can read the full story of the woman from Darlington in *The Biggest Secret* in the chapter entitled "Satan's Children". Edward Heath's name comes up again and again in research into child abuse and Satanism and, in the same chapter, David also tells another story about a woman who names Heath as a Satanist:

> "She had been brought up by a satanic family in Scotland and had been sexually and ritually abused as a child by the Scottish Brotherhood network. Her husband was also a Satanist which is why he was given the responsibility of looking after Burnham Beeches, an area of ancient groves and forests managed by the authorities in London and including an area called Egypt Wood. Late one night in the early 1970s during Heath's reign as Prime Minister, she was taking her dog for a walk when she saw some lights. Quietly she moved closer to see what was going on. To her horror she saw that it was a Satanic ritual and in the circle was the then Prime Minister, Edward Heath, and his Chancellor of the Exchequer, Anthony Barber. She says that as she watched him, Heath began to transform into a reptile and she said that what surprised her was that no-one in the circle seemed in the least surprised."

I cannot say for certain if these stories are true as I wasn't present myself. However I'd like to share something Jacob and I talked about in connection with the last story. What could we do if we came upon a satanic ritual, which we were powerless to stop in that moment? We could be present and observe it with a totally neutral energy. We could embrace it with acceptance and keep the heart open. This would automatically create a higher vibration and help to lift all those present to another level. To react with fear and panic would immediately result in our being pulled to the level of what was happening and contributing to that energy field at that level. I'm sure there are those who will protest at what I write here, but it really is my experience. Earlier in my life I have given and received very deep healing where the only "technique" used was that of total unconditional acceptance. This requires of course a very high vibrational state and this is why I so often say that enlightenment or Self-Realization is the only way ahead for this planet. Such a state is totally neutral and this energy transforms everything it touches.

So, back to the cream cakes and cappuccinos in Copenhagen. As we discussed the reptiles Jacob suddenly looked straight ahead and said, "There's one here now."

I looked in the direction Jacob seemed to be looking in and saw that one of the kitchen staff had left the kitchen and was standing in the doorway. He looked pretty normal to me and, quite surprised, I asked, "Who? The one who just came out of the kitchen?"

Jacob laughed. That wasn't who he meant at all! The one he was referring to was not in this dimension in physical form, but had appeared etherically. He had appeared in a higher vibrating energy body and Jacob could see him clearly next to the table where we were sitting. I began to be aware of a strong presence, but on this occasion did not see the reptilian being in question. Jacob was communicating telepathically and what follows is part of the message I was given.

"This being comes from a higher frequency and although he knows what those on the lower frequency want – the lower reptilians want to get rid of human beings – it is not in his interest. It is important that you, Jacqueline, tell the other side of the story – tell about the evolution of "the good"." (This is the expression that was used. Normally I do not talk about good and bad as ultimately both "sides" play their parts perfectly. However I feel that on this occasion I must use the words I was given.) "It is important to tell that not all of the reptiles are against the humans and that there is now a "breakaway group" who is working for "us". They are working with us to help prevent the fulfillment of the reptilian agenda. One of the challenges and possibilities on planet Earth is to develop a conscience and a group of the reptiles have done this and will now work for the upliftment of consciousness on the planet."

This was our first meeting with the energy I later began to call "The Ruby Red Reptile" and there is more to come about our meetings with this energy. So it seems that the higher reptilian group is now working to lift the vibrations of those on a lower level, just as many of us are here on Earth to lift the vibrations and consciousness of those who are not yet aware of their potential. I find it interesting that I moved to Machynlleth in Wales for a while in order to have a quiet space whilst writing the first edition of this book. Up until the day before I left for Wales I wasn't aware of the fact that this beautiful country has as its national symbol the red dragon! Now, whenever I see a flag with the red dragon on it I remember the Ruby Red Reptile. The dragon has been used as a very positive symbol for thousands of years. It is said to symbolize the kingly nature of the lion together with the high-flying aspect of the eagle, which represents godliness or the higher dimensions.

Something I would like to say here is, even though I talk about the Ruby Red Reptile, I am always wary of personifying energies and then talking about them as living beings. I have seen so much of this throughout the years and I actually believe a lot of what is channeled as "Ascended Masters" is simply a personification of a high vibrational energy. Ultimately each one of us in human form is simply the personification of a particular thoughtform on other levels of consciousness! I am aware that this Ruby Red Reptile could also be the personification of the collective energy field that has now lifted its consciousness and is moving upwards. This would be the sum of the energy fields of the human beings who are waking up, leaving behind old patterns of fear, control and manipulation and saying yes to the realization of their full potential. Throughout the rest of this book however, for the sake of simplicity, I shall refer to the energy that manifested in the café as the Ruby Red Reptile.

Before we finished our meeting for that day Jacob shared a couple of insights I want to pass on here. First of all he said he had a feeling that a part of the reptilian agenda to sabotage the upliftment of consciousness could be to create a parallel world – a kind of virtual reality or holographic insert. He talked about the importance of giving energy to the "real world" – really being here and being aware of what is happening and what is needed. Secondly he said he also felt that the days after the death of Princess Diana were used to try out new methods of emotional manipulation – new ways of using holographic technology to manipulate mass emotions.

Before commenting on both of these insights there is something I'd like to add. Giving energy to the "real world" also reminds me of something I heard some time ago. A psychically sensitive person who had given a public talk somewhere in Britain had commented on all the New Agers he met when he was doing his work on the inner planes. He said something to the effect that they were constantly surfing back and forth across the astral plane imagining they were doing great spiritual work! I say that everything needed for enlightenment is present- here and now – in this moment. If this is so then we can also trust that everything we need to safely steer us through the time ahead is also here. This may not sound so exciting compared with great inter-dimensional adventures but I feel it needs to be said. Great inter-dimensional adventures may still happen, but if you are also grounded in your own integrity on the physical plane you will be able to handle them. Being grounded in one dimension opens one up in a natural way to the next level.

Now let us go back to Jacob's insights. With regards to the days after the death of Princess Diana I remember what I experienced as I watched the funeral service on the television in Denmark. At one point there was a minute or two of silence and I used that time to tune in to see if there was anything I ought to be aware of. I saw a deep pinkish red color and imagined this could be the color of love and emotion blended together. This would certainly fit with the sentiments being expressed. Then almost at once the color was lifted to the area known as the "third eye" in the center of the forehead. This is a psychic center connected with manifestation, clairvoyance and vision. I watched inside and felt that this lift was forced. I didn't feel it was a natural transmutation of energies. I really felt as if something was being "done" – that this energy was being used in some way. I didn't quite know what to make of it, but the next day when I saw a repeat of the funeral service I had the same experience again. I wasn't clear about what exactly was happening but had the feeling I'd understand later. When Jacob shared his insights that day in the café, I felt my own experiences in some way supported what he said.

With regards to creating a parallel reality, remember in the previous chapter I talked about Barbara Marciniak in *Bringers of the Dawn* suggesting that "a new god to worship" could be the potential holographic insert in the time ahead. I also feel, as I know many others involved in this area do, that we may very soon be presented with some event that will demand our utmost discernment and where it may be extremely difficult even for the discerning to know what is real and what isn't. Barbara Marciniak actually says that these "new gods" will be reptiles and also warns that in the time ahead not all who come down from the skies will belong to what she calls "the family of light". She also says this will be a lesson in authority – a challenge for people to turn inwards and become their own authority.

In chapter 3 I said that one of my associates had mentioned the fact that Sai Baba and Tony Blair were different types of "aliens" and that ultimately Tony Blair was the stronger of the two. I'd like to say a little more about Sai Baba here because he is certainly offering a great challenge to those who are, or have been, his devotees. He is offering them a chance to take back their spiritual authority.

I was in India at the beginning of the new millennium and was not far away from Puttaparti where Sai Baba has his main ashram. These past few years many Sai Baba devotees have come to events I have held and have often asked me how I felt about Sai Baba. This has not been so easy for me because I have actually never felt very good about him, but didn't know why this was so. At the same time I have much respect for the guru – disciple relationship as long as it is needed and would not wish to say anything against another person's guru without good reason. So in the middle of January 2000 I decided to make the trip to Puttaparti and see for myself. I traveled there with John, a man from England who had joined me, and when we arrived in Puttaparti I said to him, "This is no Buddhafield!"[1]

Even though we were right next to the ashram I could not really feel an energy of higher consciousness in the area. The town itself just didn't feel good. The moment I got into the hotel room I became very sick and I was sick for days. No – it wasn't a deep cleansing because I was in the presence of "Baba" as some devotees would claim. I am used to being in the very highest of energy fields and this certainly wasn't one of them! After being given a homeopathic tablet from a Danish woman I was able to go along to a couple of darshans[2] with Sai Baba. The first time I saw him my stomach turned over as he walked towards me. I saw him at another darshan later the same day and became incredibly sick again and was in bed for several days, totally exhausted. We stayed in Puttaparti until I was well enough to travel and then we left.

---

[1] Buddhafield is not used here in connection with the Buddhist religion. It is a term used to describe a very high vibrational energy field in which people can experience the enlightened consciousness.

---

[2] Darshan happens twice daily at the ashram. Sai Baba comes out and walks amongst those gathered there

As soon as we left I started to feel fine again but as we drove out of Puttaparti I was suddenly flooded with images and thought-forms to do with child pornography and sexual abuse of children. At the time I didn't know why this happened. However, a few days later whilst visiting a spiritual commune in Poona I was introduced to a Spanish woman who was interested in my work. She was a therapist and told me the story of her visit to Puttaparti some years earlier. Her former boyfriend had been a devotee of Sai Baba and claimed that whilst he was a young teenager Sai Baba had misused him sexually. This had really messed him up psychologically and he had decided to go back to the ashram together with the woman I talked to and confront his former guru. She told me it was very difficult for him and, although they were at the ashram for a couple of weeks, he just couldn't bring himself to face Sai Baba and they left again. She told me that she had had the same kind of reaction I also had in Puttaparti. She felt ill and felt as if she lost her energy. She said she knew she was not in the presence of some great master and was very glad to leave the place.

The next day I was standing outside of the commune when I suddenly heard an American couple talking quite loudly. I heard the man say, "and then he told me to drop my pants."

I just knew he was talking about Sai Baba and followed them for some time. He *was* talking about him and I heard many stories of claims of sexual abuse at the ashram. I shall only write a small part of what was said and have chosen the following because it was so typical of the whole tone of what this man was saying:

> "Then he (Sai Baba) put his finger into my perineum, but
> I know he wasn't attached to what he was doing –
> Baba's beyond such things. I know he was only stimulating
> my Kundalini."

I felt like saying, "Wake up for heaven sake! If Sai Baba is the great avatar[3] you believe him to be (do they exist?) and if he can manifest ash and oil out of nothing, then he doesn't need to stick his finger up you in order to stimulate your Kundalini!"

I can see that it is very difficult for people to accept that their beloved guru is not what he or she is said to be. This can be very painful. However I decided to tell this story here because I know these things are now coming to the surface and I know there are many Sai Baba devotees who are devastated. After I returned to Europe I was actually presented with a file entitled "The Findings". It had been compiled by former Sai Baba devotees, many of whom were also devastated when they began to find out what was going on. They decided they had to publish these findings and they do certainly not make light reading! There are many stories of sexual abuse – also concerning boys as young as seven years old – and proof of deceitful dealings and faked "miracles". Sai Baba was well known as a performer of miracles and was said to manifest healing ash, gold watches and other things out of nowhere.

I would like to take this opportunity to say something here to those who have seen Sai Baba as their guru. I know this can be a very traumatic time for many but perhaps you could look at it like this: The fact that you have had a guru

---

[3] Avatar – term used for a great Soul said to manifest as a fully Realised being – a pure expression of 'God'

shows that you have been in contact with your own inner guru – what I called earlier the deepest potential within us all. You projected this out onto someone else and this is what is called a positive projection. It is fine to do this and is a natural part of the journey. There is nothing wrong with projections, positive or negative. They are simply opportunities for us to see ourselves more clearly. So keep your heart open and continue on your journey until you become one with your inner guru, inner lover, master of the heart or whatever you wish to call it. Perhaps you still need or hope to find a real teacher to guide you a little longer. If so, I sincerely hope you find that teacher.

I know there are many spiritually awake people, some quite high profile, who say they know what Sai Baba is about. They choose to remain silent at the moment in order to protect the work they are doing and I have to respect this – not everyone finds himself or herself playing such openly provocative roles. However I would like to see all those who know what is happening, in this and other areas, speaking out together and being willing to show themselves. This can be done from the heart in a non-agressive way. The sooner things hidden are revealed the sooner the lifting of the consciousness of millions is possible. I also see much energy "wasted" in criticizing those of us who reveal such things. I know of several groups and individuals who began researching the conspiracy but who stopped because they found it so "negative" and found that their "spiritual work" (or New Age business) suffered as a result.

Going back to the subject of discernment, there is one piece of advice I should like to offer here and that is to be very wary of anyone or anything which seems to promote division and this can also take the form of working for the light against the dark! Us being the goodies and the other side the baddies also belongs to the illusion of separation. This doesn't mean we cannot be discerning and creatively work to lift the consciousness on this planet. Anyone who has gone beyond the illusion of duality automatically does this. However, as I see it, I'd say that every challenge we meet is an opportunity to respond fully in the moment without losing the vision of oneness, whilst still remembering that each player in the drama is just as much an aspect of that oneness as every other player.

I also feel it is important that people are grounded in their physical bodies and are in touch with their hearts and feelings. It's important they dare to be who they are – dare to listen to themselves, feel their deepest feelings and be real. I see a danger in so many people being so caught up in the artificial feelings of characters in movies and television soaps or in interaction with others happening mainly through compuctor games. Also important with regards to being grounded physically is keeping the energy field or aura strong and not weakening it with the abuse of drugs, alcohol, too much television and microwaves etc. Contact with nature helps tremendously and so does feeling in tune with the place where you live. If you live somewhere you love it is easier for Earth to nourish you and communicate with you.

In *The Last Waltz* I wrote about NASA's Project Blue Beam which was researched by Canadian investigative journalist Serge Monast who died mysteriously just after he managed to reveal details of Blue Beam. His life was threatened several times beforehand. This project is about holographic imagery to be used to simulate the following kinds of scenarios:

- Simulation of "the end times" and a "Second Coming" where the sky will be used as a giant movie screen and groups of people all over the world will be presented with different versions of the reappearance of their particular messiah. This could include a gigantic space show using tri-dimensional optical hologram and sounds and laser projections to send out holographic images to different parts of the world which fit with the predominating regional / national religious faiths. These images of "God" will speak in all languages.
- Telepathic electronic two-ways communications using EFL, VLF and LF waves can stimulate people in such a way that each one believes God is speaking to him or her from deep within.
- Technology is also available to give certain groups a "rapture" experience where they imagine they have been taken up to Heaven, initiated or gone through an ascension process.

Project Bluebeam also talks about plans to stage an alien invasion using holographic imagery. This would give an unprecedented opportunity to create great fear amongst people and offer great opportunites for total control to "protect" the world population from this perceived threat. So I'd say that giving energy to the physical world and physical body isn't a bad idea in the time ahead! I have known of Project Bluebeam for many years but when I read V.S.Ferguson's novel, *Inanna Returns*, I was surprised to find a similar story. It seems that during the time of overt Anunnaki control of Earth there were many prophets of doom who created great fear in humans. They told of coming destruction, of earthquakes and floods and it seems people became quite addicted to being frightened out of their wits! Marduk, the evil Anunnaki ruler, learned to feed off this fear. On page 118 we read:

> "This fear generated an energy which Marduk learned to feed off of, and he began to encourage fear by projecting holographic images onto the skies, creating terrifying visionary scenes. He experimented with this fear energy, manipulating and modifying it to satiate his appetite. It was better than human flesh, and easier to manage."

As stated earlier, much of the inspiration for the above book comes from the Sumarian texts.

I recently saw what was said to be the final episode of *The X Files* where all should be revealed. I was quite shocked at what was revealed! We were told that what was behind the whole story of government cover-ups and secrecy was the fact that they knew something the Mayans knew thousands of years ago. We were told that the Mayan Calendar ends in December 2012 because the Mayans knew that just before that time there would be an alien invasion that we were powerless to stop. I was amazed when I heard this. Naturally I immediately thought of Project Bluebeam and of the fear a threat of alien invasion could provoke in people. It would also be a wonderful excuse for getting the whole population microchipped. I do feel we need to stay awake and be aware of these possibilities.

Another thing, which may be worth considering right now is this: down here on a planet where we incarnate in order to learn to use free will and to develop our own authority, it is probably a good idea to be quite suspicious of visitors coming from the skies to do it all for us! That just doesn't seem to be the game plan for life on planet Earth! I know there have been predictions of mass evacuation and help from the Sirians to make sure we make it through the challenging times ahead. I actually invited Sheldon Nidle, author of *You are Becoming a Galactic Human*,[4] to Singing Heart Center in Denmark in 1995. Sheldon Nidle has a strong Sirian connection and I felt many of the things he wrote about the Sirians and their concern for our planet were correct. However, I felt that the messages he started to give out later about dates for mass landings and large groups of humans being directed to underground cities were "off the wall"! I don't know what happened to Sheldon Nidle's contact with the Sirians and why he was given such chaotic messages. It could be that he was outwardly manipulated in some way or simply that unfinished psychological stuff sabotaged his work. Perhaps the time had come for him to become clearer psychologically so as to be as clear a channel as possible. I don't know, but whatever happened I'm not judging it. However, as the drama unfolds, I feel that any scenarios to do with rushing in from the skies and saving us and lifting people off the planet belong to the past. I'm sure this is not the way ahead.

Not so long ago I was actually reading an article about the tendency here on planet Earth to find some god to worship. The author suggested that the reason the Sirians

---

[4] In this book Sheldon Nidle reveals a plan in which the Sirians were supposed to land on Earth at the beginning of 1996 and help humanity make its way through the Photon Belt – a beam of high vibrational energy which would take the planet into the 4th dimension ready for an even greater lift in consciousness in 2012. Part of the plan was said to involve putting Earth in a holographic bubble as a form of protection until we were ready for full immersion in the higher energies. Also predicted were three days and nights of total darkness and freezing cold temperatures as we entered the Photon Belt

must not interfere is because it has been tried before and backfired. I understand it was the Pleiadians who made this "mistake" and therefore have been bound to Earth karmically for a very long time in order to help sort out the problems it caused. Humans beings began to worship them as gods, thus allowing those wishing to take control to do so as they also began to appear as gods in the skies. The Sirians mustn't repeat this – better we make a "mess" of things than they land and people again treat them as gods and give away their authority, their inner spirituality and the opportunity of initiation. I'd actually say that anything, which leads people away from the path of true Self-Realization, is ultimately not the way ahead – no matter how noble the cause. However, the Sirians seem to play a very important part in the evolution of our planet and therefore I have devoted the whole of chapter 8 to Sirius.

Some years ago I spoke with someone who had experience of the 21-day preparation process undertaken by those training to become "breatharians". Breatharianism is about "living on light" – spiritual energy or prana – instead of food. I know this is a possibility in the future, but also know that recently some who claim to have been living on light have not been doing so. This didn't surprise me as I had met some of these people some time ago in New Zealand, but won't go into that story here. However there was something I found interesting about the account of the 21-day process. I can't reveal the source of this information, but was told that part of the preparation for living on light for some people was to go through a form of psychic surgery performed by reptilians on the inner planes. The result of this for one woman was that her skin turned tough and scaly resembling the skin of a reptilian. There was apparently no change in the consciousness of the woman – just outer changes. So what has this to do with real enlightenment? Is it just another distraction or is it another form of manipulation of consciousness? I don't know.

Some people today also advocate sending love and light to the reptiles they say are manipulating from the lower fourth dimension. Ultimately I'd say do whatever feels right, however I'd prefer to see people daring to embrace their own shadow first! It's often far easier to focus on reptiles and negative ETs rather than face one's inner demons. If, in total neutrality, you can embrace your fears, "perversions", cold-bloodedness and your wish for power to dominate and control, then you have sent love and light to the lower fourth dimension. I'd say that when there is no longer any individual shadow that has not been embraced, there will be no fear-based collective drama playing itself out here in the world.

Just as those who are still into religion may be giving their power away to religious leaders and gods in heavens, I see other spiritually minded people giving away their power and the opportunity for deep transformation by projecting what needs transforming onto the reptiles. As long as any aspect of us is projected outside of ourselves we are not whole, and the search for enlightenment, wholeness or oneness will continue.

Having said this I am not trying to imply that nothing is happening outside of us. It is and it isn't! As long as there is an emotional reaction to what happens in the outer world there is also a corresponding inner process to be dealt with. As long as individual and collective vibrations are low enough to connect with the lower astral or lower 4th. dimension there will be identification and suffering on the planet. When one has cleared emotional baggage one may still meet similar situations but it is no longer the same. A role is simply being played out in the collective drama. Even if the role resembles a personal drama played out in the past there will be no real identification with it. There will be no resistance to the part being played – no goodies and baddies. This is freedom.

Many of us often repeat the fact that, as long as we are in the middle of this drama being played out on planet Earth, the best protection is to keep one's vibrations as high as possible. This is good advice, and yet all of us who have incarnated here are part of the collective energy field and can find ourselves confronted with elements that attempt to manipulate or control from other dimensions. What to do in such situations? Stay calm, don't judge, and use your love and power. Love is needed in order to keep the heart open and not to judge. Power is needed to very firmly state that you are not to be interfered with – remember this is a planet of free will.

I actually remember only two occasions where I was consciously aware of what could be called some kind of "attack". On both occasions I did not attract these attacks by being in a low energy state and share these incidents here especially because of this. No matter how high our vibration things can still happen! I feel this is an important point to make as so much New Age teaching suggests nothing can happen if you are in a state of love, positivity etc. This is just not so! As I often say, "Life happens whether you like it or not but the God inside of you is free to dance".

The first incident took place in the summer of 1993 on the night of my first meeting with Jacob. We sat in the garden talking about future ideas for work together and at one point Jacob etherically placed a golden pyramid over the center to bring in an even higher vibration. It was a warm summer evening and a beautiful meeting. Before going to bed that night I switched off the light and two very small beings suddenly flashed infront of me, right in my face, as if to scare me. I must admit I did get a shock! They looked like small demons with horns and sharp eyes. They had a bit of a "hellish" look about them and were certainly not the type of being I would have dreamed up myself. In a loud voice I told them to get out of my space and not to come back. I felt no kind of life energy in these two beings – they could even have been holographic inserts. I can best describe the energy as a kind of metallic science fiction vibration. What I feel happened that night was that I came under some kind of attack designed to scare me away from the next part of my work. When Jacob and I met we reconnected with work we had done together many times in past incarnations – work with a very specific extraterrestrial focus. I see this attack as similar to what happens sometimes when people have an extraterrestrial experience followed by a sudden visit from the "Men in Black". In *The Biggest Secret*, chapter 2, David Icke writes:

> "Many witnesses have described how the so-called "Men in Black" materialise and dematerialise when they threaten people who are communicating information about extraterrestrials and UFOs. They can do this because they are interdimensional beings who can appear in any form."

The second incident happened in Denmark in the summer of 1999. We had beautiful hot weather and I was enjoying being there and offering my work at various summer events taking place in parts of Scandinavia. One day when I was having some time off I was aware of the fact that David Icke kind of popped up in my consciousness a couple of times. I wasn't thinking about him – his face just seemed to appear for a short while. Next day I started to feel very strange and heavy, and could hardly drag myself off the bed. I was exhausted! I walked through the hallway of the house I was staying in and a woman named Jyoti, a Shaman living in New Zealand, saw me and asked if I was OK. I told her I felt as if I was dying – I really felt as if the energy was being sucked out of me. She told me to lie down and said she would read my energy. I could feel her moving her hands around in my aura and in no time at all I felt fine. When I opened my eyes Jyoti told me she had been very surprised to see that my heart was being attacked very viciously. She said I was being attacked by a huge "griffin".[5] Strange as it may seem I didn't know what a griffin was and she explained that it looked like a kind of reptile with wings. Up until that point Jyoti and I had not really had time to talk much together and she knew nothing about that part of my work which connects me with David Icke. She also knew nothing about the "reptilian agenda".

I sent a quick email off to Jacob just to double check what was happening. I didn't tell him much and didn't mention the griffin – I just said there'd been some kind of attack. He emailed back at once telling me not to worry as everything was now fine. He added that I'd just been carrying something for David for a couple of days! I later found out that David was speaking in Indonesia at that time. He had

---

[5] I later spoke with someone from England who told me that when she went to school there was a griffin on her school badge. She described it as an "old-world dragon, standing on its hind legs"

obviously been under some kind of influence from which he needed to be free in order to do what he was doing and I had "carried" the energy for him for a while. 1999 was the year David published *The Biggest Secret*, his first book to contain cutting-edge information on the reptiles, and usually the reptilian story was included in his talks.

I have recently been looking more closely at the work of Rudolf Steiner, a German metaphysician who was both a mystic and an occultist. He founded Antroposophy. I bought a book containing lectures he held in Germany in 1917 and would like to add some of his information here as it seems relevant. He actually writes that between 1841 and 1879 there was a kind of war in the higher dimensions which resulted in certain dark forces being cast down onto the physical plane. He described this war as one of many symbolically described in legends as Michael's battle with the dragon. Apparently the energies which were cast onto Earth are now actively influencing the will and motives of human beings. Steiner goes on to say that these dark forces particularly try to create confusion in such a way that humans are prevented from developing a positive relationship with the spiritual world. This, in turn, influences people at the time of death and results in them not being able to meet death in a enlightened way. I really do feel Steiner has much to say that sheds light on the situation in the world today and do recommend his lectures, especially those on the manipulation of consciousness and the misuse of occult powers.

Many people have heard of The Greys, a smallish grey colored race that often has huge saucer like eyes. Descriptions of them vary, as do descriptions of human beings. They are often portrayed in ET-type movies and television series such as *The X-Files* and are also associated with the underground bases, such as Area 51 in Nevada, USA. The Greys also seem to be connected to Orion. I understand that they are cold emotionally because they do not have a well developed feeling center and that part of their study of human beings is concerned with the study of human emotions. I remember an account of an encounter with the Greys told to me by a German woman who came to an event I held in Copenhagen. She seemed a very intelligent and grounded woman, and when she told me the following story I felt that it was true.

She told me that she was ironing one evening at her home in Germany when suddenly there was a knock on the door. Her husband opened the door but couldn't see any one outside and closed the door. There was another knock and on opening the door again he was amazed to see a group of small grey beings with huge eyes enter the house and go into the living room. The woman saw them come into the room where she was ironing and said that a part of her was astonished and another part felt it was totally natural that they should be there! The beings told them that they wanted to spend some time in the house with them in order to study their emotions. The couple agreed and allowed them to stay with them for some time.

Apparently everything was going smoothly until one evening when the couple went to bed and were about to make love. The Greys suddenly appeared around the bed! When the couple said they wanted some privacy the beings explained they would like to stay because humans experience most emotion when they make love. They wanted to be there for that experience. The couple agreed and soon afterwards the Greys left. When I met the woman in Copenhagen she said neither she nor her husband had experienced this encounter as negative and they hadn't seen the Greys since.

I know it is said that beings such as the Greys and the reptiles feed off emotional and especially sexual energy, but an encounter with them does not necessarily have to be negative. I would also say that under such an encounter it is important to be calm. Remember that Earth is a planet of free will and you have the power to demand such beings leave your space at once and do not interfere with you.

In his book *Engle til alle Tider,* Danish writer Dennis Stanfeld has the following to say about The Greys and Reptiles (I have translated from Danish):

> "The Greys: Amongst The Greys there are six main races and many subsidiary races. Most come from Orion, Rigel, parts of Ursa Major (not the Plough) and also from Draco and Zeta Reticulum.
>
> "They all have one main goal: to take over Earth and use it for their own selfish means.
>
> "Especially in the USA, they have until recently with permission from the governments, kidnapped people and animals and used them for genetic experiments."

Talking about the reptiles, he says they live inside of the surface on their own planets of origin. He also says they have always had a negative agenda on Earth and that this hasn't changed. I would ask Dennis Stanfeld to reconsider this. One thing he says about The Greys and reptiles that does make sense to me is the following:

> "One cannot say that there is any form of co-operation between them (the reptiles) and The Greys with regards to taking control of Earth. Both parts are simply too egocentric for this."

He says that the reptiles have a more destructive agenda but that both groups try to fulfil their agenda by manipulating the governments of Earth and by working with the Secret Government. Something I need to say here is, even though it would appear that there are ETs with negative agendas, I sometimes have the feeling that most negative ET experiences are government hoaxes or some form of mind control.

In her book, *The Pleiadian Agenda*, Barbara Hand Clow suggests a close link between the reptilians and Nibiru who, she says, have a similar vibration. So she implies there is a reptilian race and another race on Nibiru. She actually writes that the Nibiruans see the reptiles as gods and love the Kundalini[6] energy that flows through their spines. She says the Nibiruans are metallic biology – what we would view as "non biological" – and that the metallic electromagnetic force in their bodies resonates with reptilian sacred Kundalini fire.

Towards the end of her book is an appendix entitled "The Sirius Star System and the Ancient records of Orion." Here it says:

> "The Anunnaki are metallic beings originating from Orion, and they have great difficulty being able to feel."

---

[6] Kundalini is an eastern expression denoting the creative life force. In its unawakened state it is located at the bottom of the spine, and is described as being curled up like a sleeping snake

This also fits in with the psychological profile of those believed to be playing major roles in the Illuminati agenda: cold, unable to feel or express emotion, highly developed intellectually.

When I re-read parts of *The Pleiadian Agenda* a few days ago I suddenly remembered an interesting email I recently received. It was actually a kind of article passed on by someone and concerned the Ashtar Command. As I understand from the note accompanying it, the article consists of information from a book entitled *Mysterious Signs in the Sky* written by Israel Norkin. If you opened the book you are now reading at this page where I mention the Ashtar Command, I would understand if your reaction were to close the book again. There is so much channeled rubbish published in the name of the Ashtar Command. This particular command is said to be an intergalactic fleet run by a space being called Ashtar who, these past few years, has promised mass landings, evacuations, space ship parties for the "chosen ones" and much more! It seems that every lower level New Age channel is picking up Ashtar. I promise that what follows is not more of the same kind of stuff! The writer of the article actually says that every medium who has an astral being at his heels "immediately has Ashtar on the psychic "hook up". Here is a little of the information the writer offers us:

> "Now, so far as Ashtar is concerned, he is **not** a man, and you can tell this to your people… What is all this about Ashtar appearing in his Light body in the living room? How can he, since he isn't a man? He comprises thousands of beings making up a giant organization. He couldn't appear in their living rooms. Yes they are having appearances. They are

not hoaxes, but what are they getting? Who is it that's coming? Just because it comes through and signs itself, 'This is Ashtar' – if someone calls you from Washington and says, 'This is the Pentagon' – you don't say, 'Thankyou Mr Pentagon.' Many space beings can be Ashtar. There is no certain man by the name of Ashtar that I know of, anywhere... There is a particular group that is nothing but a group of beings who operate a gigantic mechanical brain," *(Here the writer of the email adds, "which may explain why some who claim to channel 'Ashtar' have channeled a voice that sounds mechanical or metallic.")* "a **computer**... It is one of the computers that were left after the collapse of the Galactic Empire (based in Orion). The computer is neutral... However it can be used as a tool by either regressive or progressive forces to unite their respective agendas together and also as a tool of infiltration of enemy forces who are linked to the 'collective'.

"Ashtar is a being, all right, if you want to think of a computer as a being. A computer that is perhaps twenty miles in length. Tell your people, Ashtar is a mechanical brain, but not as we think of it. It's a monstrous mechanical brain that once controlled the galactic administration of the entire Milky Way Galaxy. And the brain is **decadent** due to the regressive programming... a galactic Frankenstein's monster one might say, a creation gone awry that has been programmed to assimilate, assimilate, assimilate anything and everything. Therefore certain (regressive) ones of the Space Confederation still rely on it, inaccurate as it may be at times. It's that group, small as it may be, but large in one sense, that gives out the Ashtar information. Therefore, it can be **light** and **dark**."

The writer does say that what George van Tassel of Giant Rock, California first received was Ashtar the computer giving information to the light side, or the Space Confederation. Apparently van Tassel did not receive Ashtar later because he went on to a higher source of information. The writer states also that the Ashtar some are receiving is a force that is coming in on the astral beam from the forces of the sex and fertility "gods". If you are interested you can read the full article on: **www.angelfire.com/ut/branton/ashtar.html**.

According to Jan van Helsing, *Secret Societies And Their Power In The 20th Century*, published by Ewertverlag, George van Tassell was involved in ET contacts that some US. presidents were aware of. Apparently van Tassell was charged with sending special communiqués to President Eisenhower.

I include this information here because I feel it is useful and also because I want to stress that it seems many groups and species have tried to use this planet for their own agenda – it is not only the reptilian race. We could also say that we who say we work for the upliftment of consciousness also have an "agenda" and are therefore involved in "the game". Without sides there could be no game. I often talk about allowing the parts we play to play themselves through us without our getting identified. If we are identified we are still caught up in the drama and we keep it going. It is the energy of higher consciousness that will ultimately lift this planet beyond the drama, and that energy is neutral. I know it is sometimes difficult for people to accept what I am about to say: that ultimately any view of life which perpetuates the illusion of positive and negative keeps us locked in duality and thereby feeds this agenda which we now call reptilian. This is also why I so often talk about research into the area of the "conspiracy" being balanced with real meditation. Meditation brings one to the state of non-identification.

There are many groups in the world today who use a prayer called "The Great Invocation". The final line of the prayer is:

"Let Light and Love and Power restore the Plan on Earth."

I would suggest that the Plan here refers to the collective lift in consciousness, which awaits this planet. One thing I'd say about the reptilian consciousness is that it really challenges us to manifest individually and collectively the energies of Light and Love and Power. I use capitals here to show I mean that these qualities must be manifested in their highest frequency or potential. We need real Light – Light that shines neutrally into the darkness so we can see what is and what is not. We need real Love – a Love we could call Compassion. Compassion is total acceptance and non-judgement as it recognizes that all other aspects of the one consciousness are playing their parts perfectly. Yet it is also discerning and is not afraid to speak out and challenge an unbalanced energy to move to a higher frequency. Perhaps this is Love in its Power aspect. Power is needed to confront what needs to be confronted inwardly and outwardly. Power is not afraid to remind other aspects of the oneness that manipulation, control and taking away the freedom of others is ultimately not the way forward. Love is the law on this planet of free will.

To sum up chapters 3 and 4, I'd like to say that if I was asked to briefly say who the reptiles are and where they come from I'd probably say this: They are a race of beings which often, but not always appear, in reptilian form. Some come from other star systems and some live inside of the earth in physical from. There is also a group that operates from other dimensions – dimensions that vibrate faster than our 3rd dimensional reality and therefore are normally invisible to humans. As the energy on this planet rises, more people are finding they can see into other faster vibrating dimensions and therefore there are many reports of people seeing reptilians and the reptilian other-dimensional aspect of people they know in human form.

Research into ancient, often hidden, texts seem to show that there have been several groups of extra terrestrials who have controlled or tried to control Earth, and there are different hierarchies within these groups. Not all wish to manipulate and control Earth and its population and there seems to be a group that is now working to help free planet Earth from this control. This control happens largely through frequency control – keeping humans stuck on a very low-level vibration. Therefore, even though it can be very interesting to read historical research and discuss different theories, the most important thing in the time ahead is true spiritual development. As people individually and collectively raise their vibrations beyond the levels the reptilian controllers operate from, the control will become impossible. This is a challenge – a challenge that also offers us the possibility of planetary initiation.

Q. What do you do if you find a spaceman?

A. Park your car man!

6

Shape-shifting

Towards the end of the seventies I had a partner named Rahasya who ran some pretty intense encounter therapy groups in Denmark. I attended many of these groups with him and the group sessions would sometimes continue until late into the night. The energy was of a very high vibration. We always sat on the floor in a circle as we worked and one evening he was sitting opposite me as he took a woman through quite an intense emotional process. A couple of other woman sat close by them and I focussed gently on them, supporting them all with a meditative energy. Suddenly it was as if a veil was lifted and I witnessed a completely different scene. I saw the four of them as black Africans, almost naked and Rahasya had some kind of bone through his nose. Two of the women were stirring a cooking pot and there were banana trees just behind them. I was amazed but didn't react and just kept a gentle focus on the scene that had suddenly appeared before my eyes. It lasted for quite some time.

Later on, when I told him what had happened, Rahasya said that a couple of psychics he visited occasionally had told him about a significant incarnation he had had as leader of a tribe in Africa. It appeared I had seen beyond this present incarnation into an earlier expression of life. This particular event took place very early on in our relationship.

Later on we started to practice tantric[1] sexuality which of course took us into some very heightened states of awareness together. We would spend an hour or so every evening just looking into each other's eyes meditating. Anyone who has practiced this technique will know that this is a powerful way to open up to another person on a very deep level. Of course we experienced changes occurring as we looked at each other – different faces appeared and disappeared as we saw different sides of the personality or projected aspects of ourselves onto each other. This is quite normal. However there were a couple of faces that appeared regularly when I looked at Rahasya in this way and I later found out that they fitted the description of past expressions of life picked up by the psychics I mentioned earlier. After some time the same kind of thing would also happen when I met other people. I could look at them and converse with them on one level, but would also be watching a completely different scene play itself out on another level or dimension. I had a Guru, Osho, at that point in time and noticed that when I sat in front of him and focussed my eyes gently upon him he disappeared in no time! In a flash he was gone and only light remained – quite a clear sign, I'd say, that nothing much was happening on a "personality" level. This was always my experience of him.

There is nothing unusual about the experiences I describe here and I had actually forgotten about them until early 1999 when I held some 1-day events in Britain as a follow-up to David Icke's speaking tour. Information about the reptilian story was included in the material David had just presented and this included the topic of shape-shifting. As I

---

[1] Briefly I can explain this as the art of combining sexuality with loving awareness and meditation

prepared the follow-up days the experiences described above suddenly came back to me as something to be included in the presentation. Remember I said that the energy in the encounter groups and in our tantric sessions was of a very high vibration. This allowed me to slip in and out of 3rd dimensional reality. The vibrations on the planet today are also rising or being speeded up and therefore the veils separating different levels of reality are also falling away. This is allowing more and more people to see beyond so-called normal every day reality. For some this comes as quite a shock and I have heard that it can be a challenge for people to know what is "real" and what is not. However, I suggest that "real" here simply means what belongs to this dimension of reality. Everything a person experiences is real in some way – real in the way that it is an expression of someone's reality.

I would suggest that what I experienced in some of the tantric meditations with Rahasya was a mixture of several phenomena. It could happen, especially at the beginning of a session, that I projected some un-owned aspect of myself onto him – perhaps some feeling I was not willing to express. I remember once I was very angry with him and kept this anger hidden. I suddenly saw him as the devil with horns! This was obviously my own anger I was projecting onto him and this also explains why it is so important that people who work psychically first get to know themselves on a very deep level, and accept and embrace every aspect of themselves. If this is not done it is very easy to project these unaccepted parts out and see them as phenomena in other people and other dimensions. Sometimes I believe I saw past expressions of 3rd dimensional life and sometimes was even seeing expressions of life in other light-bodies in other dimensions. I have experienced expressions of life in different bodies, or "light-bodies" as they are called today, happening simultaneously in dimensions other than 3D. Sometimes I also saw what I would describe as "masks" belonging to different sides of the personality I knew as Rahasya. With time it becomes easier to distinguish what is what. However I would like to say here that the most important aspect of such a meditation comes when this spectacular show is over! It is not experiencing all this psychic phenomena that is the goal. If one goes deeply into such meditation all phenomena disappear and in the end there is only light – the one light or energy which flows through the whole of creation. This is seeing clearly! This is what is often described as seeing with the eyes of God.

What I say here is also relevant for people who are meditators. As people begin to go deeply into meditation there can be many interesting experiences: colors, lights, messages, angelic visions etc. These belong to the world of psychic phenomena – there is nothing wrong with them, but this is not the goal. Beyond this level we find a deep silence and a vast emptiness – a knowing which cannot be put into words. You may have heard the story of the student who runs excitedly to his teacher saying:

> "Master, Master – My meditation is deepening. I'm seeing colors and having visions and I'm sure I heard the music of the heavenly spheres."
>
> "Don't worry," the teacher replied, "just continue with your meditation and these things will disappear!"

Here is a very different piece of information – one that is also relevant to this chapter. In the previous chapter I mentioned a book called *Encounters in the Pleiades: An inside look at UFOs*. In this book there is a description of what has been seen to happen in America during a "twister" – a kind of tornado. Sometimes after such an event panes of glass have been discovered with blades of corn through them or a metal instrument can be found lodged halfway through a very solid object. It seems that the high energy vibration of a twister causes energy to speed up to such an extent that physical matter starts to vibrate faster than the speed of light and can disappear out of this dimension. When the twister is over and the energy falls back to a lower vibration, things manifest again in the physical world but sometimes in a haphazard manner.

This is the same principle we saw with the Philadelphia Experiment[2] in the United States when an attempt was made to demanifest a ship and the crew on board. The ship and crew began to disappear and then something seemed to go wrong and the experiment was stopped. Certain crewmembers were apparently found welded into the sides of the ship. One was even said to have been found in Italy with his head through a brick wall! A couple of men disappeared down a time tunnel and reappeared during a similar experiment conducted in the same area in the US forty years later. They had not aged at all during their forty years in a completely different time – space reality! When I had the center in Copenhagen several people told me they saw me begin to demanifest or saw half of my body disappear for a while. I was obviously in a very high

---

[2] Read about the Philadelphia Experiment in *The Montauk Project, Experiments in Time* written by Preston B. Nichols and Peter Moon (Westbury, New York: Sky Books 1992)

vibrational state and began to disappear out of 3D time and space.

One other relevant piece of information: I have heard David Icke tell the story of a man who took a lot of LSD back in the sixties. This particular man and his friends apparently had very similar experiences whilst under the influence of the LSD, in that they began to see certain people change into reptilian form. What they noticed with time was that it was the same people who seemed to turn into reptiles whilst others amongst them didn't. In normal day reality those who did change all seemed to portray the same types of characteristics and watch the same types of movies and so on. It seems to me that when these people who took LSD expanded their consciousness and were able to see into dimensions otherwise closed to them, they also began to see other very dominant aspects of the people around them. Perhaps they actually saw expressions of life in other dimensions, which strongly influenced the present 3D expression of life.

Psychic experience can be fascinating but it can also be very difficult for people to understand what is happening when they start opening up to other realities. It can even be difficult for people who work in this area to distinguish between one dimension and another.

One of the areas in which I disagree with some of David Icke's information in *The Biggest Secret* and the conclusions drawn from it, is when we come to the information given to him by a woman named Arizona Wilder[3]. It is also Arizona Wilder's testimony that has provoked the greatest criticism of David's work in the area of the reptilian story. She claims

---

[3] Bridge of Love has released a video, *Revelations Of A Mother Goddess*, where David Icke interviews Arizona Wilder

to be a former mind controlled slave who was programmed to be a "Mother Goddess" who could conduct satanic rituals for the highest Illuminati families on this planet. This includes presidents and other high-ranking politicians and most of the house of Windsor – the British Royal family – whom she claims shape-shift into reptiles and devour sacrificial babies. She claims to have broken away from the Illuminati and has told her story to David Icke. This seems very strange considering the fact that her two sons are said to still be in the control of the mind control department of the US government. Here is a quotation of Arizona Wilder taken from *The Biggest Secret*. She is refering here to Queen Elizabeth II.

> "I have seen her sacrifice people and eat their flesh and drink their blood. One time she got so excited with blood lust that she didn't cut the victim's throat from left to right in the normal ritual, she just went crazy, stabbing and ripping at the flesh after she'd shape-shifted into a reptilian. When she shape-shifts she has a long reptile face, almost like a beak, and she's an off-white color."

I really feel there is either misinformation, misinterpretation or both here. It was not easy for me to write this part of the story as I have much love and respect for David Icke and his work. In 1998 David asked me to read his first draft of *The Biggest Secret* which was written before he met Arizona Wilder. I read it and felt it was an important book – especially his research into the murder of Diana, Princess of Wales. I felt it was a book that could awaken millions of people to what is really going on in the world – and perhaps this is still so. I hope so.

In November 1998 I joined David in America and we held a workshop together in Sedona. It was at this point in time he had been put into contact with Arizona Wilder and was going to go to L.A. to meet her for the first time. After the Sedona workshop I was to spend another week in America before flying on to New Zealand. Someone actually gave me a free plane ticket from Phoenix to Los Angeles, so it would have been very easy for me to accompany David and a couple of other people when he went to interview Arizona Wilder. However, I didn't go with him – I just seemed to lose my physical energy and made no attempt to go anywhere. It was almost as if I just wasn't meant to go and I spent a week alone in the apartment near Phoenix. So I have never met Arizona Wilder. My first reaction on seeing the video David made with her was a strong feeling that, a lot of the time, Arizona Wilder was quoting from David's book. It was as if she had memorized relevant passages and was quoting them back to him in order to seem to confirm his research. I know that this video provoked a strong reaction in many, and there were great debates that went on in magazines and on the internet between those who condemned the Arizona Wilder information and those who supported it.

I do not have a problem at all accepting the reptilian influence and the fact that shape-shifting can happen. I just do not feel comfortable with Arizona Wilder's accounts of what she says she has experienced. However I have read about the research that has been done into shape-shifting and I understand that human beings also have reptilian DNA – just as we have a reptilian part of the brain. Those who shape-shift are able to shift the DNA to reptilian form and then manifest it on the physical plane. Those with a strong reptilian influence apparently are more reptilian than human in their genetic structure. David Icke writes about a woman named Christine Fitzgerald – a close confidant of Princess Diana – who told him that the Windsor's wanted to interbreed with Diana's genes because they were becoming too reptilian and could end up having trouble maintaining a human form in the generations to come. A long time before this information came to David, Jacob actually said that one of the reasons Diana had been married to Prince Charles was because the Windsors wanted to make use of the great amount of light there was to be found in her genes.

An interesting perspective on shape-shifting can be found in Ivan Fraser's *Truth Campaign* – edition number 14 – in the fourth part of a series entitled "Beyond the Veil". Ivan says that it is actually an insectile group which is mainly behind the manipulation of consciousness, but that this group often choose to manifest in reptilian form as this is a form which humans fear. Activation of this ancient fear makes possession very easy and, as Ivan also writes, the demonization of the serpent in "Judeo-Christianity" has given the demonic predators from the astral plane a convenient form through which to manifest and prey upon humanity. I'd like to quote a passage from the article, as it seems relevant to this chapter on shape-shifting:

> "Demons are usually seen by those with extra sensory vision as variations on reptilian creatures, usually with insectile characteristics (the other main human phobia), as well as many variations on other fear symbols: cats, bats, priests etc. In fact, almost any combination of characteristics is possible created from the fear thought forms of the mind of mankind over thousands of years. A robed humanoid lizard is a classical

manifestation of demonic consciousness upon the lower astral plane, created from: the Judaic idea of the devil as a lizard and the robed human representing the Church which has created enormous amounts of terror via religious persecution for over two thousand years. Another characteristic of these thought-forms is their ability to shape-shift into various fearful images in response to the mind that is witness to them; usually the witness is psychic."

David Icke says there are three types of reptilians. First of all there are the "full-bloods" – that is true reptilians who simply hide in a physical form. Then there are "hybrids" who are said to be a reptile-human crossbreed. Lastly is a type who can manifest directly in this dimension but who cannot hold that state. He claims that leading Illuminati families such as the Windsors and the Rockefellers are full bloods and that they are fully aware of this and of the agenda they are helping to implement.

One of Arizona Wilder's claims is that shape-shifting Royals lose control at the scent of blood and physically transform back into reptilian form. Jacob's response to this was:

"What a good job none of the women at Diana's funeral had their periods – it would have been a disaster!"

Yes, we can also joke about it, but with regards to the information she has given I should like to offer some comments and insights. I do not claim that all of what follows here is 100 per cent correct, but do feel it deserves consideration – especially in the light of what I wrote at the beginning of this chapter. What I share here is a mixture of

Jacob's feedback after studying the Arizona Wilder video, feedback from a very clear seeing person I'm connected with in New Zealand and my own insights. There are also a few lines from a lady who did a very unexpected and wonderful Tarot reading in Australia. There is more about this reading in the chapter entitled "Royal Command Performance." What feels important here is all of us sharing our knowledge and insights in order to sort out what is really going on. Who actually said what is not so important, and with this in mind I simply share our different comments as separate quotations, in italics, without adding names. I hope some of this is of use to people who are also trying to understand what is happening.

Looking at photographs on David Icke's website:
"Arizona Wilder is being used. She's giving much misinformation. She's not clean – there's also darkness there. William F. Buckley is reptilian beyond belief! Prince Michael Stewart, Count of Albany is very dark."

Doing some energy work to free David of a reptilian attack:
"We need to put mirrors around Arizona Wilder to keep her in her own energy while we try to help David. The reptile that has hold of David by the neck, is connected to Arizona Wilder. We must now try to get her to let go of David. I've never met such an aggressive energy before – it could actually be one of Arizona Wilder's other light bodies. She's giving misinformation so that the Royal family will appear just as dark as she is."

With regards to Zechariah Sitchin, author of books on the Anunnaki. Arizona Wilder accuses him of being present at and taking part in satanic rituals she has conducted and of being a

> shape-shifting reptile. Here is the response of one of us who read Sitchin's energy field:
> "There is a lot of reptilian energy around him – especially around his head. There's darkness in his mind but there is light around the rest of his body. This could be because Sitchin works with the reptilian energy and writes about such matters. This makes it easy for thought forms about the reptilians to be caught up in the mental aura."

I know there are people who say they have seen reptilian energy around David Icke. In such cases I would suggest several explanations: 1) That what I've just written above also applies in this case; 2) David is sometimes under reptilian attack. I know this has happened and together with Jacob helped to clear him from one attack. Jacob and I both had strong abdominal pains for a day or two after this clearing. 3) Some people are really getting caught up in this reptilian stuff and are projecting reptiles all over the place! This doesn't mean that the reptilian story is not true, but it is also bringing with it a lot of nonsense.

> "Arizona Wilder is extremely clairvoyant. She channels what she sees without realizing that some of it is happening in another dimension. She does not have multi-dimensional sight."

> "We must remember that Arizona Wilder plays an important role. Let's not give all the power to "the conspiracy"! David could just as well have been planted to create a lot of fear on the planet right now."

> Thoughts shared by many at the moment:
> "If this manipulation of consciousness has been going on for

so long, why suddenly allow David and Arizona to put out all this information right now? They are both being used."

Discussing The Biggest Secret:
"All the misinformation is coming from this woman (Arizona Wilder). There's a kind of madness around her. There's real darkness and misintent directed at David. This woman has such awful power. The book will be saved. The right information will be put there in the end – the wrong information must be taken out."

"The Queen Mother could come from Kusku. She has light bodies many places – also with the reptiles. Perhaps Arizona imagines the energy she sees with the reptiles is the Queen Mother in physical form".

"It's also completely OK that Arizona Wilder tells what she thinks she sees."

On the subject of time travel and the Royal family:
"With regards to the Royal family of Britain you can walk into their 'house' and imagine they are not there, but they are there. They go to their 'place', (a different dimension) do what they do and come back. They come back fortified in their 'reptilianness'. They have to do it because everything needs a battery and that's their battery. Arizona probably sees it and thinks it's happening down here." *(More about time travel in chapter 7.)*

"The British Royals are not Satanists on the physical plane. They used to be, but are not any longer."

> *Talking about those of us who have a job to do regarding the reptilian agenda:*
> "Each morning in meditation I check which level I'm on to make sure my energy hasn't dropped. These guys seem to be getting worse and the only protection is to stay on an energy level above the one they operate on. Just by hearing their names over the telephone, I see people's faces changing as they do in films. Yes David's book will also be ridiculed, but what's around that's normal any more?"

Arizona Wilder also names Sir Laurence Gardner as a shape-shifting reptile and Satanist and this has caused quite an outcry from people who have read his books and respect his work. I would like to see David Icke, Sir Laurence Gardner, Zechariah Sitchin and Arizona Wilder come together publicly and discuss these issues.

And finally, to conclude this part of the chapter, a few words from Jacob. I feel what he says is important here because I do feel that misinformation (both negative and positive) concerning the reptiles and other extraterrestrials is being used to divert attention from what is really happening in this dimension.

> "It is important that people concentrate on the politicians. Satanic abuse and such things are really happening amongst politicians in 3D."

Around the time of the solar eclipse in August 1999, David Icke and Arizona Wilder put out information about Illuminati satanic rituals that would take place. I accept this happens and feel the best we can offer is to use every possible opportunity to lift the energy vibration to the next level. Here is a paragraph taken from a short article I sent out over the internet at the time of the eclipse. We could say it's just another way to shape-shift!

> "At an eclipse (like at the time of the full moon but even more so) the possibility for accessing higher dimensional energies for planetary enlightenment and the possibility of accessing energies to reinforce the lower dimensional energies which still to a large extent control the planet, are both intensified. The Sun's magnetic fields are not effecting the planet so strongly and therefore it is easier for dimensions to merge. What of course is important is what is accessed and what it is used for. My advice to people I generally work with is meditation – tuning in to the highest possible and anchoring that energy on the physical plane at this point in time. In some of the latest information being put out about the force controlling the planet, we read about "reptilian shape-shifting" at times of the full moon and eclipses. People report seeing politicians and royals at satanic rituals turning into 9ft tall reptiles. What I feel is happening here is that those working with lower 4th dimensional energies have an even greater opportunity to access the malevolent energy that keeps this planet at a low vibration. This is often done through satanic ritual. I feel that those who can see physically or clairvoyantly, see the lower 4th dimensional energy or reptilian body being contacted and experience it as a 3rd dimensional reality.
>
> "However people can just as easily use full moons and eclipses to access higher consciousness. I have actually recommended 'shape-shifting events' at the time of the eclipse: people shape-shifting into their highest potential! This message may sound funny, but I ask people to remember that what I really mean by

this is being in a very high-energy state – a state of purity, meditation etc. Some would talk about 'accessing your multi-dimensionality'. Shape-shift into who you are in your most enlightened state! Otherwise my message to people who are not able to stay in meditation and hold a high vibrational energy in that way is this: dance, sing, chant, celebrate – whatever keeps your heart open and keeps you vibrating with the energy of joy and love is fine. Don't get caught up in fear, negative thinking and scary ideas. Stay in the heart, not the head."

I feel this message is still relevant today and in the time ahead.

7

Visions in the jungle

At the beginning of 2002 I was invited to accompany a researcher, whom I will call Andreas, on a trip to Equador. He was doing research into plant medicine and was also interested in the visionary substances that are used in shamanic ritual in order to gain insight into the medicinal properties of plants. When Andreas told me about his expectations for the trip I suddenly remembered something I was told several years ago during what turned out to be a very accurate psychic reading. I was told there would come a time when it would be important for me to visit indigenous people in many parts of the world and take part in some of their ceremonies. I was told I should simply drink what they drank, smoke what they smoked and I would thus gain information that would be important for my work. So when I was invited to visit shamans in Equador it felt right to do so and I accepted. It would be my first visit to South America.

I was told that we would be meeting shamans who would introduce us to ayahuasca – a visionary brew drunk throughout Western Amazonia. The brew consists of two plants that are boiled together for hours. One plant contains the hallucinogenic substance dimethyltryptamine, also secreted by the brain with no effect whatsoever when swallowed. This is because the stomach enzyme monoamine oxidose blocks it. The second plant contains substances that inactivate this stomach enzyme so the hallucinogen reaches the brain. Ayahuasca has been drunk in parts of South America for centuries.

We could ask how people from a so-called primitive society, with no knowledge of physics and chemistry, knew these two plants should be combined in order to make the brew. Researchers say that it was probably not discovered through experimentation as there are too many possible plant combinations – over 80,000. Jeremy Naarby has written an excellent book on ayahuasca entitled *The Cosmic Serpent – DNA and the Origins of Knowledge*.[1] In it he debates the supposition that nature is conscious and comes to the conclusion that shamans gain a lot of their knowledge through direct communication with plants. The first time he heard that someone in Peru had learned of the medicinal properties of certain plants by drinking a hallucinogenic brew he thought the person was joking! Later however many Indians shared their knowledge with him and told him that the source of this knowledge was the ayahuasqueros (shamans who drink ayahuasca). Ayahuasca was actually referred to as "the television of the forest"! It was said that through ayahuasca one could see images and learn many things.

With regards to nature being conscious, I remember one of our talks with Credo Mutwa. He was talking about the fact that every cure and every aid human beings need is found in nature. Nothing is missing. He said that it was almost as if Mother Nature knew human beings would end up on this planet and that they would get sick. She has provided everything we need.

---

[1] Published by Tarcher Putnam

In his book, Jeremy Naarby says that several botanists had written of their ayahuasca experiences over a hundred years ago, but that the first subjective description to be written by an anthropologist was published in *Natural History Magazine* number 77 in 1968. The article, entitled "The Sound Of Rushing Water", was written by Michael Harner. In the middle of this academic article, Harner described how, for several hours after drinking the brew, he found himself in a world beyond his wildest dreams. He met bird-headed people and dragon-like creatures that told him they were the true gods of this world. He had many powerful visions and at one point, when he felt almost sure he was dying, he saw that his visions came from "giant reptilian creatures" found at the lowest depths of the brain. Harner's work was generally discredited because of the fact that he wrote about these things but he had many more experiences with ayahuasca. Here is a passage from an account published in 1980:

> "First they showed me the planet Earth as it was eons ago, before there was any life on it. I saw an ocean, barren land, and a bright blue sky. Then black specks dropped from the sky by the hundreds and landed in front of me on the barren landscape. I could see the "specks" were actually large, shiny, black creatures with stubby pterodactyl-like wings and huge whale-like bodies... They explained to me in a kind of thought language that they were fleeing from something out in space. They had come to the planet Earth to escape their enemy. The creatures showed me how they had created life on the planet in order to hide within the multitudinous forms and thus disguise their presence. Before me, the magnificence of plant and animal creation and speciation – hundreds of millions of

years of activity — took place on a scale and with a vividness impossible to describe. I learned that the dragon-like creatures were thus inside all forms of life, including man."[2]

So over the years botanists and anthropologists have published their experiences with ayahuasca and there are also websites dedicated to the subject. What I read led me to wonder if ayahuasca could help me gain more understanding of the reptilians. At the beginning of the book, *The Cosmic Serpent*, is a quotation from Heraclitus:

"Those who love wisdom must investigate many things".

This expresses the motivation behind my decision to go through the experiences I write about in this chapter. I participated in seven ayahuasca ceremonies and what follows is a summary of my experiences. In order to protect the identity of the shamans involved I have used fictitious names.

The last day of February 2002 Andreas and I had our first meeting with Don Carlo, a mestizo shaman who would guide us through our first ayahuasca experience. The following day we met with Don Carlo, his son and a couple of his son's friends at Café Amazonas in Quito ready to depart for the jungle. We arrived late in the afternoon and made the final preparations for the ceremony. I say the final preparations because we had already been preparing for several days. Participants should follow a special diet avoiding salt, sugar and fat, and should abstain from sexual relations and alcohol for several days. The diet consisted mainly of fish and bananas, which are rich in serotonin, a

---

[2] Michael Harner *The Way of the Shaman*, New York: Harper and Row

neurotransmitter in the brain. Apparently long term use of hallucinogens diminishes serotonin.

Shortly after sunset we were given a cup of ayahuasca which we blessed and drank. It tasted extremely bitter – like the most bitter grapefruit juice you could imagine. We knew that drinking ayahuasca usually caused violent vomiting and diarrhoea. A huge storm was about to break out so we had to hold the ceremony on a covered, stone-floored area that had three walls and an opening out into the jungle. We were actually given plastic bags to vomit into incase we couldn't make it outside in time. After drinking we sat down against a wall and waited. Before travelling to Equador I had not been well and was still feeling quite weak due to high altitude sickness in Quito. I closed my eyes and tuned in to the spirit of ayahuasca and asked her to be gentle and protect me. I had heard people could have very violent experiences during these ceremonies and knew that ayahuasca could be hard on the physical body.

I could hear heavy rain beginning to fall and it seemed to be preparing the way for some experience I could only surrender to. I felt vulnerable and yet safe. I was aware of a roll of thunder and a few flashes of lightning and I could feel my physical body beginning to shiver and shake even though I was not feeling cold. I could hear Andreas beginning to vomit into his plastic bag and was happy I didn't feel sick at all. I was sitting in a half lotus meditative position and had my focus at the third eye chakra in the middle of the forehead. Suddenly I saw my former Guru, Osho, standing in front of me. I felt myself lift off through the top of my head and move upward through the cosmos. I heard the voice of Osho:

"Show people the stars, Jacqueline. Let others do the other work."

I knew this refered to my work. It refered to what could appear to be a conflict between my deeper work, which could "show people the stars" and facilitate an opening into higher conciousness, and the urge I also felt to speak about the manipulation of consciousness and many of the subjects included in this book.

I had many cosmic visions and experienced much bliss. It seemed Andreas was having more difficulty surrendering to the process. When he wasn't vomiting he would try to speak to me. I remember short sentences such as:

"The time is now 10.52"

or

"We have now been here 2 hours and 43 minutes"!

I was aware he was trying to stay in control in some way and just let him be, but actually found him quite disturbing at times!

Time passed, and as the storm grew stronger and stronger the thunder and lightning seemed to hurl themselves at the flimsy structure under which we sat and the jungle lit up appearing like a scene from the movie *The Perfect Storm*. I heard Andreas vomiting violently at the edge of the covered area where we were gathered and suddenly he called my name, asking me to come and help him. I got up to help, but I seemed to be without legs and as they gave way under me I collapsed onto the floor! Don Carlo picked me up and sat me against the wall again. He told me he would look after Andreas. Some time later I also vomited a little and then felt the diarrhoea coming on and managed to get outside. What a powerful experience it was to sit outside in the pouring rain and feel the jungle pulsating around me. I felt at one with the spirit of Mother Nature and of ayahuasca and I was very aware of my cosmic origins.

Early in the morning I saw a heavy grey shadow hanging near the ceiling and later found out that others present, who also saw it, described it as a "predator". One of the things we talked about the first time we met with Don Carlo was the predators many people claim to see hovering around during shamanic ceremonies. We asked Don Carlo if there really were such things and his reply was:

> "The predators are real. We can only be free of them if we are on the energy level above them."

This has been my message all along in connection with the reptilian consciousness. I would say that the prolonged use of ayahuasca, or any other hallucinogenic substance, could ultimately weaken the system and open one to possession by such entities.

The next evening brought us our second ayahuasca ceremony at a place near Santa Domingo de los Colorados, and our shaman was a very wise, politically active Sachala Indian. I was very sick during the ceremony but Andreas was even sicker than I was. I felt quite concerned about him but we could not really help each other and just had to go through the experience. The visions were again cosmic and I spent most of the time in communion with the energy I knew as Osho. Of course this energy is also an aspect of myself. When I was able to stand up again and go out under the stars I saw beautiful electric blue lights darting back and forth across the landscape. Later I was able to get a little rest and at sunrise we were invited to the shaman's room for a talk. I had amazing insights holding crystals and artifacts that had been used in shamanic ceremonies for many generations and seemed to be in direct communication with the spirits and memories of the objects. Resting in a hotel room later that day, I had the feeling my introduction to ayahuasca had been very gentle and that there were far more powerful experiences waiting for me. This feeling proved to be true.

A few days later, after some much needed rest and nourishing food, we took a four-seater plane from El Pujo to a place deeper in the jungle. We had been flying for some time and I was enjoying an amazing view of the Amazon when I saw our guide struggling with the door of the plane. It seemed the door was not closed! He opened the door right up and tried to slam it closed a couple of times. As I sat there watching I felt that if it hadn't been for the sight of the jungle below I could have imagined I was just sitting in a taxi! We finally touched down safely on what looked like a football field, ready to spend a week with the Ketchwa Indians.

Don Anton was our next shaman. He was just visiting the area, but agreed to do a ceremony for us because the shaman we had really come to see was away on a trip. He was a very gentle old man with a beautiful presence and, as the ayahuasca was beginning to take effect, he began to sing a most haunting melody. It seemed ancient – as ancient and mysterious as the jungle surrounding us. One at a time, Andreas and I were called up to sit with him as he sang and performed shamanic work on us using large feathers and rattles.

During this ceremony I saw the snakes. I saw giant luminous serpents and seeing them reminded me to ask the spirit of ayahuasca if I could be given more information about the reptiles. It was as if ayahuasca showed me that I did not really need more information. I was told it was okay to write the next edition of the book, *Only One Sky To fly In*, but I was advised not to spend too much time doing so. I was again reminded to "show people the stars".

When the visions began they had a different quality from the previous evenings. It was as if they descended on a thick colorful tapestry and everything I saw was permeated with the same underlying pattern as if cut from the same fabric. I could even describe it as a kind of paisley pattern. The visions could be cosmic, jungle-like or sometimes, when Andreas disturbed me with his chatter, they could be very ordinary. It depended on which frequency I was tuned in to. He really disturbed me at one point and I came crashing down and saw a group of people sitting at a McDonalds restaurant! Yet always I saw the same dotted fabric that reminded me a little of the Aboriginal art I had seen in Australia.

There is a beautifully illustrated book entitled *Ayahuasca Visions – The religious iconography of a Peruvian shaman*. It is put together by Luis Eduardo Luna and Pablo Amaringo. Amaringo says his paintings show only what he himself has seen on ayahuasca. When Jeremy Naarby showed the book to Peruvian shamans they showed an immediate interest and said their own visions were very similar. This is also how I felt when I later looked at the paintings. It seems that either a certain kind of vision is found within the plant or that a substance in the plant activates a certain quality of vision found within each human being. There is a striking similarity between these paintings and Aboriginal art and both are also reminiscent of images connected with DNA and molecular biology. There are dotted and zigzag staircases, snakes entwined, double helixes, twisted vines, ropes and what looks like DNA in its spread out form. In his book Jeremy Naarby mentions the similarities between Australian Aboriginal and Colombian Amazonian stories about the creation of life. Apparently both talk about a cosmic snake whose powers are symbolized by quartz crystals. At the end of this chapter I write more about the conclusions he comes to in his book.

Some of the details in the paintings resemble sketches I have seen from ancient Sumaria and Babylon, especially those that seem to symbolize the entwined strands of DNA. One such sketch is depicted in Sitchin's book, *The Lost Book Of Enki*, page 128. It is said to depict the double helix DNA emblem of Ningishzidda, a son of Enki. There are two dragon-like figures each holding a stave and in between the staves are two intertwining serpents. The dots in all of the figures resemble the patterns of DNA in its spread-out form and as I said earlier they also remind me of the underlying patterns I saw in ayahuasca visions.

In Joseph Campbell's work on world mythology there is a volume entitled *Occidental Mythology* where Campbell includes a sketch taken from Mesopotamia around 2200BC. It shows a serpent ruler sitting on a throne and at each end of the sketch we see the double helix. I would say that when one puts all of these pieces of information together it is impossible not to imagine that there is a link between extraterrestrial serpent-like "gods", DNA and the creation of life on planet Earth.

I was very, very sick during this ceremony – we both were. I was aware of an old Indian woman, the shaman's wife, regularly taking my pulse. She was tiny and yet she managed to help me up and away from the hut each time I needed to vomit. I felt a deep contact with my inner body wisdom and it seemed to be telling me that too much ayahuasca could be very dangerous for the physical body. I have later learned that people have died during such ceremonies and I do not write this chapter to encourage people to take ayahuasca. I would really urge caution. I was exhausted at the end of this ceremony and was too weak to stand up and thank our beautiful shaman when he came to say goodbye.

We spent a few days resting in the jungle waiting for the other shaman to return. I enjoyed the simple life – eating with the family we stayed with, bathing in the river and relaxing in a hammock. I loved the heat and the intensity of nature. I only knew a few words of Ketchwa but one day, whilst practicing the Ketchwa greeting, I had a real surprise. Several people were passing by as we lay in hammocks and I remember repeating the greeting, "Ali Punja", as each one passed. Each person replied with, "Ali Punja". Finally a young Indian woman came along. As I was about to greet her she looked at me and said, "Er det dig der taler dansk?"

I was amazed to hear her ask me in Danish if I was the person who spoke Danish! She was apparently married to a Dane and spoke the language quite fluently. There was also a young boy who spoke some French and, with the help of the two of them, I was able to communicate to a certain extent and have a good idea of what was going on around me. Our guide spoke very little English and Andreas picked up quite a bit of Ketchwa.

Don Salenos, our next shaman, returned from his trip. That evening we found ourselves sitting on a wooden bench under the stars, clutching our plastic bags as we waited for the ceremony to begin. I felt extremely vulnerable that night. By then I knew how powerful ayahuasca was and was experiencing the toll it could take physically. Suddenly many people started arriving, including the Danish speaking woman, and we found out that the whole village gathered for an ayahuasca ceremony a couple of times a week. We went through two ceremonies with Don Salenos and what follows is a summary of them.

As with all my other ayahuasca experiences they were very cosmic and I always experienced much love and bliss. I seemed to head straight for the stars each time and especially felt connections with the Pleiades, Sirius and Andromeda. I moved freely between the higher worlds and the Earth plane and sometimes seemed to be given a kind of wand to facilitate this movement. It showered stardust and had the feeling of the kind of wand used by Tinkerbell the fairy in "Peter Pan and Wendy". The message was always of oneness – the one consciousness pervading the whole of creation. Each evening there was the beauty of the song of the shaman and the power of the individual shamanic work done on each of us present. I was also aware of the fact that I was tripping and hallucinating at times – something I hadn't experienced since my hippie days back in the late sixties and early seventies. This happened only when I opened my eyes and had to go out into the jungle. This state was very different from what I experienced lying down with closed eyed.

There was something I was uncomfortable with during the two ceremonies with Don Salenos: there were many vampire bats in the area where he lived. Large and menacing they swooped down over us, as we lay uncovered on a patch of grass near the ceremonial hut. Lying there alone at one point, I was close to being attacked physically as I was too weak to muster up the psychic energy necessary to put a protective shield around myself. As they were in physical form a lot of psychic energy was needed to keep them at a distance and Andreas arrived back from his visit to the shaman just in time to help me psychically put up the shield.

One thing I was shown on the first evening was the movie in which we play our parts. It was as if multitudes of dramas were projected from a giant kaleidoscope and the question that came to me was, "Whose hand turns the kaleidoscope?" In response to this question I was shown a shield. It was a shield of dark magic that was being used to trap us in a very low-level movie. As I was looking at ways of dismantling this shield I was reminded of the power of mantra[3] as a tool for such work.

I was also aware of many snakes and reptiles. The snakes appeared before me in very earthy and very cosmic colors. They were enormous and sometimes one would appear right infront of my nose and look into my eyes. Some of the reptiles stared at me, breathing heavily and I felt their slow vibration. I felt them deep in the bowels of the earth and deep in the consciousness of each human being. I had a vision of a well with a ladder reaching down into the depths and another leading out of the well and up into the sky. I saw that the ladder represented the spinal column along which the seven chakras or energy centers are found. The top of the well or the middle point on the ladder corresponded to the heart chakra. The reptilians I was

---

[3] Mantra is the science of repetition of sacred sounds

experiencing belonged to a level deep inside of the well. I was reminded that snakes and reptiles are all part of the collective memory and that especially the consciousness of the reptiles mostly belongs to the lower chakras.

I was shown that there was a time, long ago, when the collective consciousness of humanity was not much more advanced than these lower chakras, and therefore these energies formed the major part of human reality. Today the consciousness has evolved and we access much more of our potential. However the other aspects are still present. From the astral planes they can be, and are being, purposely manipulated through black magic and technology in order to keep people trapped at a low vibrational level. A couple of months later during my final ayahuasca experience I was shown a cage or net that seemed to be woven from a kind of heavy brown metal rope. I was told that this symbolized the prison in which humanity was caught.

I was also shown the depth of my own individual memories and experienced a deep feeling of anguish I knew many years ago. It is still there deep inside – part of the human condition – in the same way that collective memories remain. However when we lift our vibrations we are no longer identified with the shadows of the past even though they remain in the memory. I can no longer really distinguish between personal and collective memory.

Towards the end of the second ceremony with Don Salenos, Andreas and I both experienced some strange happenings and later felt there had been some kind of black magic directed towards us. This is not at all unusual in the Amazon. There are rivalries between the different shamans and many of them are extremely powerful. We were both aware of things touching us physically and could see what looked like dark shadowy substances flying in our direction. These were not hallucinations. I was aware of a very heavy energy that seemed to descend and put a lid on my crown chakra. For a while I felt subjected to someone else's reality and was relieved when we were able to stand upright and walk back to the hut we lived in. I could then settle into my own vibration. I have later learned of people who have had astral entities attached to them during ayahuasca ceremonies. I actually know one of them and would say that this person is still in quite a state emotionally even though it is about a year since his experiments with ayahuasca.

Once more I really advise caution in this area and would say that the ability to be able to hold a very high vibration is the greatest protection. However, even if one has this ability, one should not underestimate the adverse physical effects prolonged use of such a substance can have. I say prolonged use of because I know physical healings have also taken place for people drinking ayahuasca.

In his book *The Cosmic Serpent* Jeremy Naarby tells us he only really had one experience of ayahuasca. However, this experience touched him so deeply it led to years of research into the connection between shamanism and DNA. He also says that Michael Harner, the anthropologist mentioned earlier in this chapter, made a connection between ayahuasca visions and DNA. He wrote that at the time of his visions (1961) he knew nothing about DNA but later on could see a connection.

I would like to share some more passages from the book as they make real sense to me after my own experiments with ayahuasca.

Naarby says that when he started his shamanic research he already knew that the "animist" belief (i.e. the belief that all living beings are animated by the same principle) had been confirmed by the discovery of DNA. (After years of meditation and spiritual seeking, I also already knew this from my own inner experience.) He was fascinated by a theme found in mythology all over the world – that of twin creator beings of celestial origin. He mentions the life-creating twins in Yagua mythology and another example is that of the Aztecs' plumed serpent, Quetzacoatl and his twin brother Tezcatlipoca. They are both children of the cosmic serpent Coatlicue. Suddenly Naarby discovered that in Aztec the word coatl means both "serpent" and "twin". Again we see the connection between the cosmic serpent and the "gods" coming down from the heavens and creating human beings through the twin/double strands of DNA. In chapter 6 entitled Seeing Correspondences he writes:

> "I rushed back to my office and plunged into Mircea Eliade's book *Shamanism: Archaic techniques of ecstasy* and discovered that there were countless examples of shamanic ladders on all five continents, here a 'spiral ladder' there a 'stairway' or 'braided ropes'. In Australia, Tibet, Nepal, Ancient Egypt, Africa, North and South America, the symbolism of the rope, like that of the ladder, necessarily implies communication between sky and earth. It is by means of a rope or a ladder (as, too, by a vine, a bridge, a chain of arrows, etc.) that the gods descend to earth and men go up to the sky."

Later on in the same chapter Naarby writes:

> "I was staggered. It seemed that no one had noticed the possible links between the "myths" of "primitive peoples" and molecular biology. No one had seen that the double helix had

symbolized the life principle for thousands of years around the world. On the contrary, everything was upside down. It was said that hallucinations could in no way constitute a source of knowledge, that Indians had found their useful molecules by chance experimentation, and that their "myths" were precisely myths, bearing no relationship to the real knowledge discovered in laboratories."

He ended up accepting that shamans can take their consciousness down to the molecular level and gain access to molecular biology. Having seen the correspondences between twins, serpents and ladders, he wrote:

"There is a last correspondence that is slightly less clear than the others. The spirits one sees in hallucinations are three-dimensional, sound-emitting images, and they speak a language made of three-dimensional, sound-emitting images. In other words, they are made of their own language, like DNA."

I know that nature is conscious and that she can teach the secrets of creation. On my sixth ayahuasca experience I felt an urge to begin making sounds. They were rhythmic sounds with a beat that reminded me a little of something I had heard in connection with a Native American ceremonial dance. I felt as if the sounds I made were the equivalent of the dotted, serpent-like images I had seen. A shaman later told me that in advanced stages of ayahuasca experiences people sometimes begin to sing the song of DNA.

So I see ayahuasca's deepest message as being that of oneness and of the creative impulse which descends from the heaven worlds, the stars or the higher dimensions. This impulse or potential is found in the DNA of everything in creation. The ancient wisdom – the true spiritual pathway throughout time, has always known of the Kundalini energy, which, in its awakened state, relinks us with our full consciousness. The symbol for the Kundalini has always been the serpent. Anyone who opens up to higher consciousness begins to see these correspondences. Many of us have taught these Truths for lifetimes. It is an exciting time we are now moving into as science, through research into DNA and other areas, begins to bring proof of these Truths.

8

The Missionary Position –
reptilian style

One subject I must write about in connection with the reptilian agenda is that of religion as it is seemingly one of the most powerful and successful tools for manipulating consciousness on this planet. When I watched *The Reptilian Agenda* in which David Icke interviews the Zulu shaman Credo Mutwa, I was truly astonished to learn about the role extra terrestrials seemed to have played in preparing for the missionary take over of parts of Africa. I was amazed at some of the stories Credo Mutwa told, and yet what he said made so much sense! Here is the part of the story I feel is relevant right now. It is taken from the second video: Credo talks about the Chitauri, a reptilian extraterrestrial race with a very negative agenda. He has first hand experience of this group of beings and shares much information including many well-kept secrets that he now chooses to reveal. From what he says it seems that Africans were actually prepared to accept the Christian missionary takeover of large parts of Africa, and that similar preparations took place in North America. If this is true, and I believe it very possibly is, then we can certainly see that religion has been one of the most effective weapons for creating subservience, guilt and "divide and rule".

Credo Mutwa tells about a strange race of people who were seen just before the missionaries arrived. Apparently some of those aboard the Portuguese ships sailing around the Cape of Good Hope also saw these beings. They were described as being about eight feet tall, slender and chalk white in color. Sometimes they seemed to only have one leg. In African art they were often depicted in white chalk, such as in white chalk masks. I also find it interesting that certain African tribes – I remember especially the Masai of East Africa – often stand on only one leg. I also remember that the Kikuyu of Kenya painted their faces with white chalk for their circumcision rituals. Perhaps this is some sort of a leftover from the times of the visits of these strange beings who seem to have been perceived as very sacred.

These beings often wore long hooded robes of antelope skin, often the black sable antelope, and would disappear into underground caverns. They wore cross-like ornaments of gold and silver on their chests and in this way prepared the Africans for what was to follow. Such beings were also seen by the North American indigenous people before the colonization of America by the whites began to take place. When the Native Americans saw the crosses on the sails of Colombus' ships they saw them as sacred symbols. It was a similar story in Africa where the African people often accepted and protected the Christian missionaries even though they themselves were supposed to be fighting the colonists.

Credo Mutwa gave many examples of how great and respected African rulers just accepted the Christian missionaries even though they treated the Africans very harshly, destroyed their culture and undermined their rulers. He tells of the warrior, prophet and Zulu king named

Shakar who welcomed the white missionaries to his empire in Natal. Before his death he apparently warned his half brother never to attack the whites and told him to allow the missionaries to operate freely amongst the African people. These missionaries converted people to Christianity and had great power over them, behaving like dictators. They mistreated the African people and stole their land using the name of Jesus Christ to justify whatever they did. The true history of these people and much indigenous knowledge was lost and they were often forced or tricked into parting with precious relics and artifacts. Often an African who fell sick would only be allowed into the missionary hospital if he or she agreed to be baptized as a Christian and to surrender ancestral artifacts. Credo tells the story of the time this happened to his grandfather who was taken to a missionary hospital after a serious accident in a wagon. He refused to be baptized and part with his family treasures and left the hospital. An Afrikaner who asked for nothing in return later cared him for. Credo Mutwa went on to tell of a quite recent visit he made to a well-guarded warehouse near London Docks. Apparently this warehouse belongs to the British Museum and contains cupboards full of priceless African artifacts collected by the London Missionary Society.

Rudolf Steiner seems to confirm another story told by Credo Mutwa. Credo told about the vaccinations forced upon African children and said that after they were vaccinated children began to loose the ability to see into the spirit world. His grandmother tricked missionaries into thinking her grandchildren had been vaccinated – she roasted grains on the fire and then pressed them on the arms of the children. This was very painful but it left a scar that looked like a vaccination scar. When I bought the Rudolf

Steiner book[1] I mentioned earlier in this book I did something I often feel to do with a new book – just opened it at random and read the first passage my eyes fell upon to see if there was any particular message in it. I opened the book at a lecture given by Steiner in Zurich on the 6th November 1917. In this particular lecture he says that in the future there will be attempts made to make people think that anything spiritual is crazy! (I translate loosely here because the book I bought is in Danish.)

> "They will try to do this by developing vaccines against it. Just as vaccines have been developed against sickness, certain vaccines will be developed that will effect the human body in such a way that it will be impossible for the soul to give room for spiritual tendencies. They will vaccinate people against the tendency to have spiritual ideas. They will at least try – they will try to vaccinate so that already in childhood people lose the wish for a spiritual life."

Another effect of Christian divide and rule tactics in South Africa can be seen when we look at the fact that converted black Catholics were not allowed to mix with converted black Protestants. The missionaries also forbade converted Christian blacks to have anything to do with non-converts who were called "heathens". If church-going blacks had anything to do with these non-converts they were severely punished. Credo's grandfather would not allow his daughter (Credo's Mother) to convert to Catholicism and she could not therefore marry Credo's father who was a Catholic convert at the time. Because of this Credo Mutwa

---

[1] *Individuelle aandsvaesener og deres virke i menneskets sjael* (Forlaget Jupiter, Odense 1986)

grew up as an outcast – a bastard. As I said earlier I do recommend these video interviews with Credo Mutwa as they really give a completely new angle on the colonization of Africa and other parts of the world.

So, it seems that the extraterrestrial race or races controlling this planet have used religion for thousands of years to disempower and enslave humans. Being persuaded or threatened into giving away one's own light, dignity and authority to some supposed divine being has been a very effective way of keeping control of human beings and hindering their true awakening.

I have recently read an interesting book written by Cat Panther from Denmark. The working title in Danish is "Hemmelig Menneskets Liv" and the English title will be something like "The Secret Life of Man". Cat Panther traveled extensively on the astral planes and was able to come back and write about her experiences. She describes the hierarchies she discovered there whose only purpose is to prevent people from reaching the enlightened state. She describes the "departments" which carry out this agenda and the largest and most effective department is that of religion. Many may find her book disturbing but it is well worth looking at by those who wish to explore the energies behind the manipulation of consciousness here in the physical world.

Throughout time there have been enlightened ones who have brought Truth to the world and their teachings in their pure form have, and continue to, set people free. However, it seems that each time such a light came here and left behind a way to move through the illusion, the teaching was later used to imprison people even deeper. Organized religions were formed, part of the teachings omitted (such as the

Christian rejection of reincarnation) other parts twisted and plenty of myth and empty ritual added. The Truth at the core of most of these teachings is pure and it is one. There is only one sky to fly in. Today we are many who have incarnated at the same time to bring this same Truth to humanity. As we move into the energies of Aquarius it becomes a group effort. It is more difficult to crucify thousands of "messengers", but the religious indoctrination of the masses is a powerful tool and those who can show the way out of the prison of religion are still being ridiculed.

A book I recommend, *The Book Your Church Doesn't Want You To Read*[2] is actually a compilation of articles written by various people. I'd say that anyone with even a slightly open mind would have to seriously reconsider the teachings put out by the Church and other religious institutions after reading this book. Here's an example. Most of us have heard the story of the life of Jesus. We are told he was born to a virgin with the help of the Holy Spirit, thus fulfilling an ancient prophecy. After his birth a jealous ruler threatened his life and his parents had to flee to safety with him. Angels and shepherds were present at his birth and he was given gifts of gold, frankincense and myrrh by wise men. He performed miracles, was seen as the savior of mankind and was put to death on a cross between two thieves. After descending into hell he rose again and went to heaven. Did you know that exactly the same things were said about an eastern savior god 1,200 years before the birth of Jesus? His name was Virishna.

There are many savior gods with similar stories and some of those listed in the book include: Khrishna of Hindostan, Buddha Sakia of India, Odin of Scandinavia,

---

[2] Edited by Tim C. Leedom (Kendal / Hunt Publishing, Iowa, USA, 1993)

Tammuz of Syria and Babylon, Hesus or Eros and Bremrillahm of the Druids, Thor of the Gauls, Gentaut and Quetzalcoatl of Mexico, Fohi and Tien of China, Prometheus of the Caucasus and Mohammed or Mahomet of Arabia. There are many more.

The book also contains fascinating details of the myth of "the Son on the cross" and after reading what is written one is left in no doubt that the real title should be "the Sun on the cross". In *The Biggest Secret* David Icke actually has a chapter with this title and the chapter itself is a very fine resume of myths related to different religions. "Why the Sun on the cross?" you might ask. Apparently the basis of all early religions was the Sun, worshipped on different levels depending on the level of awareness of those involved. The majority worshipped it as a symbol of light and life but there were others, the high initiates, who knew more about the Sun.

They knew of the electromagnetic energy the Sun generated and the power this energy has to affect consciousness and to bring changes into the lives of those on the Earth. They also knew that the times when there was greatest Sun spot activity were times when it was possible to use the energy created for whatever purposes they wished. In chapter 12, "Bill and Ben the Flowerpot Men – Leading Humanity up the Garden Path", I actually write that it seems the Gregorian Calendar was manipulated into place so we could have the Millennium when we had it! Just as we can use Sun spot activity to lift consciousness through meditation, earth healing ceremonies and other such activities, it can also be used to create greater fear and chaos by whipping up expectations of disasters.

The Book Your Church Doesn't Want You To Read describes the ancient symbol for the Sun's yearly passage through the

12 signs of the zodiac. It shows the zodiacal circle on which we today draw up an astrological chart or horoscope, and on top of the chart is a square or cross dividing the circle into 4 equal parts. In the middle is a smaller circle symbolizing the Sun. So there we have it – "the Sun on the cross"! It is the story of the Sun as it moves through the different signs of the zodiac and here are just a few examples which will surely remind you of stories you already know.

Around the 21st – 22nd of December, the winter solstice, the Sun "dies" as it reaches its lowest point of power.

© Irene Christensen Instituttet
^/s Petersson's Trykkeri, Svendborg

However three days later it is "born" on December the 25th – the birthday of many Sun kings and saviors throughout time. At the spring equinox around March 25th the Sun enters the sign of the ram or lamb, Aries. Long ago lambs were sacrificed at this time in order to appease the gods, especially the Sun god, so that sins may be forgiven. I'm sure the idea of the lamb being slaughtered so our sins may be forgiven rings a bell for many readers.

Sun kings were often depicted with long golden hair, like a lion's mane, symbolizing the rays of the Sun. This is the archetype of the sign of Leo, which is ruled by the Sun. Samson (son/Sun) was such a king and, according to the story, his hair was cut by the woman Delilah. She symbolizes the passage of the Sun through the house of Virgo, the virgin/woman. The Sun passes through Virgo after Leo just before entering Libra, the autumn equinox, where the strength of the Sun begins to diminish, just as Samson's diminished after Delilah cut his hair. And so it goes on – stories of the Sun. Most people do love the Sun and many of us are still real Sun worshippers at heart. Just as the Sun can give light and enlighten, it can also blind us if we do not protect our eyes. If only the truth of the power of the Sun had been used to enlighten people instead of blind them!

In connection with *The Book Your Church Doesn't Want You To Read* perhaps a follow-up could be written entitled *The Truths Your Church Doesn't Want You To Know*. This came to me as I read an article about the late Dr Michael Wolf author of the book *Catchers of Heaven*.[3] Dr Michael Wolf was a top US scientist who claimed he had worked 25 years for the American satellite government. He was said to be at the

---

[3] In the US order through Dorrance Publishing, tel: 0412 288 4543 In the UK through *Nexus* Magazine, tel: 01342 322 854

cutting edge of clandestine scientific discoveries and shared much information about UFO cover-ups and ET reality. I quote a couple of passages from the article. They show the implications revelation of this information could have for those still stuck in religious belief and those still wishing to manipulate minds through religion.

> "He briefed four different American presidents on the ET reality. Jimmy Carter was keen to end the UFO cover up but when told of the religious implications he backed down. I attended this meeting. Carter had strong Christian beliefs. When told that religion is man-made and probably unique to this planet he broke down in tears."

Later on I read something very interesting concerning the Vatican.

> "The Vatican are especially worried over these forthcoming announcements. They have asked the American government to hold back, especially on the religious question, so there is more time for them to prepare. Dr Wolf said the Pope has changed the Roman Catholic view on God. 'Their future line will be "we are not in the image of God but our souls are!"'"

I really like that one! How could they hold on to the biblical creation myth if suddenly people started seeing so many different types of species? Dr Wolf says that some ETs call God "The Forever" and that they describe this force as "the creator behind everything in the universe". He also describes Jesus Christ as being of joint ET/human heritage and says he was sent to Earth in an attempt to end human violence.

I was taught that the word "religion" actually means, "to bind back" in the sense of reconnecting someone with "God". The word "bind" feels quite appropriate here as, for me, it conjures up a feeling of being unfree – of being bound. Throughout time the chains of religious dogma have enslaved billions of people on this planet and they still continue to do so. Here are two more examples of the limitations of religion:

On a recent visit to California I switched the television onto the Christian Broadcasting Network (CBN) -a channel founded by Pat Robertson. I was curious to see this channel as David Icke mentions Pat Robertson in *Children of the Matrix* – chapter 16 entitled "'Spiritual' Satanism and 'Christian' Conmen". This title gives an adequate description of the information David Icke presents in this chapter.

The program on the television was all about sin. That didn't surprise me. Promoting fear of judgement is a very effective way of controlling people. A story was told about King David's misdeeds and about some other guy who apparently refused to sacrifice an animal even though "God" demanded this be done. Instead he listened inwardly and followed his conscience. It was said that King David had done many bad things and murdered many people, but that he repented and so was forgiven. However the man who disobeyed "God" was the real sinner – he committed a much greater sin when he refused to sacrifice the animal! All kinds of quotations were used to back up this argument. In *Children of the Matrix* David Icke actually says that the original term for "sin" in the Bible relates to disobeying the will of "God" – "God" meaning the gods.

Just this evening I heard on the radio news that orthodox Jews in Jerusalem are seeking to impose seven-year prison sentences on women who prayed aloud at the Wailing Wall! Such bits of news tend to bring me back to the reality of how much light still needs to be brought into the area of religion. It is coming. There are many who do wonderful work building bridges between organized religion and real spirituality. I see this work as very important at the moment as not all people are ready to go totally beyond religion.

I remember my first real spiritual awakening – my first taste of enlightenment. Any leftover ideas I had at that time about the value of religion fell away and I saw religion for what it was. Pointing in the wrong direction, it was Truth turned inside out – upside down! I also realized the Truth at the core of all teachings brought to the world in the past by those with an enlightened consciousness. It is a great step forward when someone dares to leave behind religious conditioning and embrace true spirituality. This is really freeing up the spirit – this is coming home.

Something comes to me whilst writing this: We often use the expression "a free spirit" about people who dare to follow their hearts and follow their dreams. Can you imagine a "free spirit" who was really into religious dogma and the fear and judgement it brings with it? Recently I met a young Dutch couple about to set out on a trip around the world. They had put together a book of inspirational poems that they were selling to help fund the trip. On the inside cover was written, "Some follow a belief. Some follow a dream."

I love it! Let us also remember that every religion, no matter how repressive, has also had its own mystical tradition. There have always been those who somehow found a way through to Truth. We have had Christian mystics, Sufis and whirling dervishes from the Islamic tradition and many others. These traditions followed the path of the heart and that will always lead people to freedom. As I've said many times before, never underestimate the power of the heart. No matter how dark the alley you may seem to have got lost in, no matter how great the deception or the manipulation, the heart is always there waiting, calling you home.

Here are a few quotations that seem to fit this chapter.

- "Identifying the true nature of "the one god" beyond the age old interference here of mere "demi-gods" is the greatest challenge of our times and the only way in which humanity will fully empower itself."

    I received this in an email from Simon Peter Fuller – Wholistic World Vision: **www.globalvisions.org/cl/wwv**

- "...the unnamed God of modern Christianity evolved through Imperial intervention. He is certainly not the God of Jesus, for this God was a sublime discipline of self-awareness that dwells within everyone and needs no bridge-building pontiff to lay down the rules of access."

    Genesis of the Grail Kings *by Laurence Gardner.*

- "*Question:* You seem to have little use for religion.
    Answer: What is religion? A cloud in the sky. I live in the sky, not in the clouds, which are so many words held together. Remove the verbiage and what remains? Truth remains."

    "I Am That" – *Sri Nisargadatta Maharaj*

- "Overdose of religion will scar you for life."

The Reverend Brian Boyd of the Presbyterian Church of Ireland wrote this week to criticise Express columnist Topaz Amoore for her liberal attitude to drugs.

Among his arguments was the old chestnut that cannabis is the gateway to harder abuse. Bit like the Church, really. You start off wanting somewhere nice to go when you die. Maybe you like the words to Jerusalem. Or the outfits. Or Harry Secombe.

You start experimenting with a few mates at Sunday School; a bit of Deuteronomy here, a few proverbs there. Next thing you know you're lecturing your children on who they can marry, taking contraceptive advice from a bloke who has never had sex, making moral judgements based on superstition and prejudice or believing there is ever such a thing as a Holy War.

- "Organised religion. Just say no, kids."

Written by Martin Samuel — *Express* — 7th April 2000

- "Don't let worry kill you. Let the Church help."

Announcement in a Church magazine:

In July 2002 I was in India and towards the end of the journey spent a week with a very wise man together with whom I created a project entitled, "Free God From Religious Fanaticism". To protect his identity I simply refer to this man as Maharaji and what follows is an article I wrote for a magazine.

Free God From Religious Fanaticism

> When the world as we know it shatters
> When we have nowhere to go except the unknown
> Then we will either be given something new to stand on
> Or we will be taught how to fly!
> *(Source unknown)*

Perhaps many readers have already seen the above quotation. I received it in an e-letter at the beginning of this year (2002) and unfortunately cannot remember where it came from. However it is a wonderful quotation. The same day it was sent to me I actually used it at the beginning of a Satsang I held in Copenhagen and then went on to tell people about a very inspiring talk I heard many years ago. It was a talk entitled "You need no platform to stand on", given by Michael Barnett of the Wild Goose Company. I do not remember much about the talk but I have never forgotten the title and actually used it as a chapter heading in my second book, *Knock Knock, Who's There?*

In the Satsang I talked about the platforms many people choose to stand on – consciously or unconsciously. Platforms are false identifications – identifications with parts of the personality which, ultimately, are not who we really are. Some people identify with work or social status, some with certain characteristics that seem to work for them in society, or with their political leanings. Many still identify with a religious belief – often the one they were born into. If one really wishes to come into Truth these false platforms have to be shattered so we can stand freely as that which we really are – and who we really are cannot be expressed in words. I often call this "being centered in nothing".

Astrologically at this moment in time the planet Saturn is making its journey through the sign of Gemini and has been opposing the planet Pluto in Sagittarius. The platform being pulled from under many people's feet is that of their belief system. The belief system I wish to focus on in this article is that of religious belief. As the planet Pluto journeys through the sign of Sagittarius the whole subject of religion and religious fanaticism is brought to light. Pluto is the planet of deep transformation – death and rebirth – and during such a process the shadow is always brought to the surface before the transformation takes place. One of the keywords for Sagittarius is religion – the shadow side is religious fanaticism, dogma and holy wars. Right now we see the shadow side surfacing as we witness one conflict after another that has its roots in religious differences. As I write this I remember something I once read many years ago about religious fanaticism. It was something like, "If you don't believe you will be saved by my redeemers blood, I'll drown you in your own"!

Pluto takes many years to complete its journey through Sagittarius and as it now reaches the halfway mark I feel the time has come to move on from religious fanaticism to the next phase – transformation. On a recent trip to India I was visiting Maharaji. During one of our talks together I told him about a saying often used by David Icke: "God save us from religion". Maharaji enjoyed this saying, just as I do, and then he said that what we really need to do is to save God from religion and from religious fanatics! We talked a little longer and it seemed that in no time at all we had together created a vision – a project we wished to bring to as many people as possible. The title of this vision became "Free God From Religious Fanaticism" – FGFRF.

I know that many readers of this article have left behind religion and religious dogma. Many are the new teachers and visionaries of the future. What is perhaps useful for those who have work to do in the field of belief and belief systems is an understanding of the difference between religion and spirituality. As stated earlier, Sagittarius, ruled by Jupiter, is the sign connected with belief and dogma. The sign of Pisces, ruled by Neptune, is associated with spirituality and real spiritual experience. Pisces and Neptune speak of the mystical experience, of communion with the inner divine nature and of oneness.

I feel one of the greatest differences between religion and spirituality is that religion focuses on the outer – an outer doctrine, someone out there who interprets the doctrine, someone out there to worship. Answers come from outside, from an outer authority even though one of the greatest teachings of the Christian religion is "The kingdom of God is within you". True spirituality focuses on inner experience or realization – on inner authority. Answers come from within. Religion is belief orientated and spirituality is based on knowing. Religion seems to create separation often leading to a kind of "My savior's better than your savior" complex. Is this much different from "My Dad's bigger than your Dad!"? I saw an interesting video of a lecture given by Russell Targ where, at one point, he also talked about religious fanaticism. He actually said that most religious wars had been fought over which software we use to plug us in to the "psychic internet". Imagine us reaching a time on this planet when all people can agree that this is so!

The further one progresses on a true spiritual pathway the faster the differences disappear. Through inner experience people come to the same realization and there is nothing to fight about. In fact there is nothing really to be discussed. Instead a deep silence and knowing surfaces and in this state every aspect of creation is embraced.

I was recently interviewed for a two-hour radio program in Denmark. It was given the title "Free God From Religious Fanaticism" and during the interview I told about a kind of temple – a place of worship for all human beings – created by Maharaji. I described how the centerpiece of the temple is a divine flame. This flame represents the One God, all gods and goddesses, the Universal Power worshipped by all religions. It is the symbol of Truth, the symbol of Shakti or consolidation of the power of all gods and deities worshipped in all religions. In an article about this temple it says:

> "This is a place where you can worship in your own way and call your own God in the flame of an oil lamp! You can see your God in the way your mind wishes. This is the only place of worship on earth where the Universal Nature is represented in the flame as the effulgent idol of your concept of God."

I said to the interviewer that it seemed people were free to project any deity they wished onto this flame for as long as they needed to do so, and that they were free to worship or perform ceremonies in keeping with their particular pathway.

The interviewer asked many questions – two of them I would like to repeat here:

1. Why do you actually use the word God in this project? It has such negative connotations for many people. Why not use another more neutral word?

2. Why is there a flame in the temple? If the divine is an inner state is it really necessary to have an outer representation?

Looking at the first question, I would say that this project is for the whole of humanity, not for a chosen few. We could say that those who have come so far on their journey that they do not need to give the Divine a name or form do not need this project. They may be inspired by our work and find some creative ways to contribute, but they have their own inner experience and do not need help in removing the platform! It seems appropriate at this point in time to respect the reality of the majority of people who still use the word "God". Then perhaps many people can move on together from that point. Regarding the second question I would suggest that many people still have a need for some kind of form or structure. It is not so easy for them to relate to nothingness. A story illustrates this…

I have a friend in Sweden who has a studio for color therapy. It is a very pure place and is of a very high vibration. I remember something he told me the first time I went to visit him. The colors he had used in the various rooms were clear and vibrant and there was much space everywhere with hardly any other form of decoration. However he told me that initially people coming to the studio had often become nervous because of the apparent emptiness – so much so that he finally decided to hang a few things on the walls and place a few magazines on the table in the waiting room and consultation room. The result was that people found it easier to relax. It was very difficult for most of them to relate to nothingness! It is the same with the temple. People are used to having something to project their inner God nature onto and without something may not be able to relate to the message being given. This is natural for part of the journey. However the message of FGFRF is acceptance of and understanding of the nature of these lesser forms such as religions, gods and goddesses and other personifications of Shakti or the Universal Power. The message is that every prayer, mantra or invocation, no matter who or what it is directed towards, is ultimately an attempt to connect with this Universal Power – call it God Force if you wish – that pervades the whole of creation. In the difficult times facing humanity it is only this force which can protect us, and we are also that force.

Let us also remember that the goal of all pathways is the same and it is the same impulse that moves people to reach out for something beyond the limits of the personal self. FGFRF will work to offer many more people a direct experience of this Truth, which has been the reality of some for a long time. As heart chakras open and people have a direct experience of oneness, feelings of separation and fears about paths different from our own will disappear. There is no room for them in this new reality.

Maharaji and I imagine there may be groups and individuals who would like to creatively contribute to this project in the time ahead. You are very welcome to contact us. As I travel in the world I invite Visionary Groups to come together and share ideas and inspiration. I also hold and encourage meditation retreats, as a meditation retreat is always a wonderful opportunity for a direct experience of who we really are. It is an opportunity to allow the false platforms or identifications to fall away and enable the true light of Self, God, or whatever you wish to call it, to shine through.

The 16th October 2002, I came across an interview in the newspaper *USA Today*. It is an interview with Mexican singer Carlos Santana who, amongst other things, talks about religion and spirituality. I chose this passage as a suitable ending for this article.

> "I like spirituality, not religion or politics. Religion turns into 'My god's bigger than your god; therefore, you're a heathen, and you should die, and I'll take your land and build a temple on top of your flattened house.' Religion is corrupt business.
>
> "Spirituality is like water and sun. When it rains, the prostitute and the pope get wet just the same. Spirituality is not memorizing the Koran or the Bible while hurting people in the name of Allah or Jesus or Buddha or oil. We are all chosen. Surely we have the capacity to transmute anger and fear into a masterpiece of joy."

9

Embraced by a reptile

As I finish the second edition of this book, it has been suggested I write about a recent event in my life in order that others may see how what I experienced can actually happen. I have pondered over this suggestion and now feel I should do as suggested. I will keep this chapter brief and have changed the name of the person involved and other details.

I would say I have a good intuition but, when it comes to people, I also have a tendency to be naïve. When I meet people I often seem to tune in to their full potential and usually presume I can trust them. This has caused a few difficulties throughout the years but what happened last year was a bit of a shock! Here is a very brief outline of the story.

As I was weak physically and needed some kind of treatment, I was introduced to an alternative practitioner named Martin. He was said to have exceptional gifts and he treated me professionally for some weeks. We later spent time together sharing inspiration for a project we believed may be of value to a group of people involved in organic farming. We traveled widely together in connection with this project. There was also a strong physical attraction between us and we had a sexual relationship as well as what I perceived to be a friendship.

Martin was quite a genius but I soon saw how difficult and eccentric he could be. However, when I looked at his astrological chart, I made allowances for him. Saturn and Pluto were opposing each other in the heavens and were creating very difficult situations for the whole of humanity. Their opposition coincided with the September 11th attacks in the US. They were also activating a challenging part of Martin's chart and I believed this was throwing him off balance. Both of these planets tend to bring out the shadow sides of those under their influence. Both move slowly in the heavens, therefore triggering effects that can last for a couple of years. So I decided to be patient and not judge the strange behavior he showed at times. I also made allowances because of stories he told me about very traumatic experiences in his past. I am no longer sure all of these stories were true!

The second time we made love something very weird happened and had I been in a stronger state of health I would probably have walked away afterwards. However I was still receiving healing treatments and was very exhausted. As we made love he suddenly turned quite rough and began hurting me. This is not the kind of energy I would normally allow close to me at all in a personal relationship. It all happened so quickly it caught me off guard, but before I could really say anything I felt Martin change physically. His body became hard and scaly and so did his penis. The energy in the room changed and I pushed him away. He made no attempt to continue and I lay in the dark wondering what had happened. I had written a book on reptiles and touched upon subjects such as shape-shifting. Could this really be happening? A part of me still doubted that there was such a thing as shape-shifting and it was certainly not something I went around looking for! Looking back on this episode I actually feel that I shifted frequencies and experienced Martin on a different level. I am also pretty sure a non-3D aspect of him came closer to the fore and I experienced it.

I could not leave the room that night, as the city where we were staying was not safe. Finally I fell asleep. Next morning he took the whole thing very lightly, laughing a little at my concern. He was very caring and loving and told me that, because I was still so weak, I was not myself and was imagining things. I stayed with him. As I write this I am aware of the fact that it is very strange I stayed in this relationship – even though it was only for a couple of months – and that I put up with many of the things that happened. Something just doesn't seem to fit. I also seemed to lose my will and, even though I was receiving what were supposed to be very powerful healing treatments, I was getting weaker and weaker. I do not wish to go into much detail about what happened during the time we spent together but I can say that some of the situations I found myself in just didn't seem to fit with the rest of my life at all!

Back in Denmark, towards the end of this relationship, I was sorting through a box of old tapes and found an astrological reading I had received in the early eighties. It was a reading by an American astrologer who had devised a whole new system of astrology and I remembered the reading had been very accurate. I listened to the tape again. The astrologer actually talked about the time when Saturn and Pluto would oppose each other in the heavens and, even though these planets were not making any challenging aspects to my own chart, he warned me about terrorist attacks in connection with long distance travel. I had not experienced what is usually understood by "terrorist attacks" on my travels, however I thought about the positions of Saturn and Pluto in my own chart. I could see that, with these two planets in the positions they are in, I could experience some kind of destructive hidden agenda from someone with whom I appeared to be in relationship. There had been a kind of psychic terrorist attack in connection with long distance travel!

Let us now look again at what are said to be typical reptilian qualities: ritualistic, aggressive, hierarchical, emotionally cold, extremely intelligent. As time went on Martin displayed all of these traits. I remember someone I spoke with in California who told me that reptilian types could be very cool and detached emotionally, unless emotion is specifically directed at them. This was exactly how Martin was. He was extremely detached and also expected others to be so, yet if someone triggered emotion in him he would explode. Several times I saw him rant and rave and bang on walls. He would become abusive verbally and I also saw him display much aggression towards people. I was amazed at how cold he could suddenly become and how he could lie to people and use them to get what he wanted. As a professional he was totally unethical and, with time, I could see that no-one could safely tell him anything in confidence.

I also noticed his ritualistic behavior. We spend quite a lot of time in a place where hot water was often in short supply and yet he always had to soap and shower three times when he got into the shower. He used a bar of soap every couple of days. There were times when he reminded me of the obsessive-compulsive character played by Jack Nicholson in the movie *As Good As It Gets*! Things always had to be done in certain ways even though there were no sound reasons for doing so. I remember he told me that he did things his way and that he would never change anything.

He was also very aware of rank and educational status and always used his title when introducing himself. This often appeared strange to me when I considered his otherwise very radical behavior. He was extremely intelligent and spoke many languages. I know that several people we met felt intimidated by the enormous amount of knowledge he possessed and by his way of presenting himself.

Strange things transpired over a period of about three months and I actually had a dream warning me against him. I had continued to make allowances for him because of the very challenging astrological influences he was under. Then I began to discover lies and intrigues. I discovered he was playing people off against each other in a very smart and cunning way. He didn't seem to imagine any of these people would ever talk with each other about what was happening. As time passed he seemed to be on a mission to undermine me and make me doubt my sanity! He told me outrageous lies about people as if he was telling me things in confidence, at the same time asking me to keep these things secret. He pretended he was telling me the truth about people because he felt I needed to know what they were doing and saying behind my back. He seemed to be trying to sabotage certain relationships – some of them important for my future work.

I realized this man did not really know me. If he did he would not imagine I would keep secret the things he told me. I realized he had no idea of the kind of honesty and integrity I was used to in relation to those with whom I was connected. He also had no idea of my level of consciousness and would say strange things such as, "I can't tell you otherwise you'll freak out."

How could he imagine I would freak out! He had used me for some purpose. Someone told me that, when being in relationship with me proved to be a nuisance with regards to what he wanted to do with a certain group of people, he actually told them he had to stay close to me in order to be able to get a share of some funding I was expecting.

A certain turn of events meant that I ended up spending more time with him than originally planned. This proved to be beneficial. If I had not spent so much time with him I would probably not have discovered what he was really up to and would have given him funding that was actually supposed to be for my own work. I would have given it because I believed he needed it in a hurry for an important project. I have since heard that part of the strategy of the reptilian agenda it to filter resources away from what is important.

One day I was speaking with a friend who has strong psychic abilities. I was telling a little about what had been happening and he suddenly said that Martin had a great deal of reptilian energy that he was especially used to putting out onto women. He had apparently attempted to do the same with me and I was told it was important he learned that he must not do this in relation to me. When my friend said these things I had not told him about the "shape-shifting" experience. I later learned that a well-respected psychic somewhere else in the world had told Martin that he came from Nibiru. I believe this to be true.

With regards to people I allow to come close to me I have learned from this experience; I will never again make allowances for something that doesn't feel right. It does not matter how difficult someone's past has been or how challenging the present astrological influences are. There can be no such excuses with so much at stake here on this planet. With regards to Martin I would like to say that he played his part perfectly, just as we all do. I believe I also saw his light and hope it surfaces again when Saturn and Pluto have finished their work. I hope something of our meeting touched his heart.

10

Royal Command Performance

Thursday 21st.October 1999 I am listening to a program on the radio where listeners are sending in their response to the fact that the Chinese president was given a state reception by the Queen on his visit to England. People were protesting because of the bad reputation the Chinese government has as far as human rights are concerned. Many listeners were apparently very surprised that "Her Majesty" would entertain this person and asked how it was possible for her to do such a thing.

In September 1996 I was traveling in California for a couple of weeks together with David Icke. One morning we got into the car to drive up the coast from Santa Barbara and David suddenly fell back into the seat and started breathing heavily. A very powerful and positive energy filled the car and I simply sat and watched for a while thinking that David had gone into a spontaneous "rebirthing"[1] experience.

Then I felt the special chakra just above my heart chakra activated. This chakra, sometimes called the Thymus or Higher Heart Chakra, was whirling powerfully and the energy from it seemed to be pouring down my arms and out of my hands. After a while David began to speak and I realized I should write down what was being said. When he finished speaking I was so touched the tears were streaming

---

[1] Rebirthing is a powerful therapeutic breathing technique

down my face. I felt such compassion for whatever was expressing itself through him.

I have much experience of energy and know that the energy in the car that day was of a very high and pure nature. I don't want to analyze what was said or to pretend to know why it happened or if it was important. Please just read it for yourself. There are a few holes where I couldn't hear exactly what was said. The energy introduced itself as "The All Seeing Eye" which is often, but not always, used as a symbol for the "Illuminati" or controlling force on the planet.

Santa Barbara – September 1996

"I am the All Seeing Eye. I relinquish my power. Those who are under me will continue… it's all they know.

"My vehicles do not know love. They are aspects of me. I have seen the illusion of my desires and now have to witness the collapse of my dream. You have the power to speed the change. Now I have withdrawn from my vehicles they will become very confused and lack the clarity of thought and vision, which has been so effective in turning human beings into slaves of my desire. As a result of my withdrawal from the pyramid the bricks will quickly start to slide. The platform, the stage, is now yours. I hope the consequences of my actions will not prove so catastrophic as the pyramid of my creation crumbles and falls. I wish you well. I only wish it were not necessary…

"America appears to be the center of global power. It is merely a smoke screen for where true power lies. The diversion. The people of America are victims of London. London is where the true power lies. It lies in the energy field

of what is called the United Kingdom. It is that power, that
natural power, twisted beyond measure that allowed that small
stretch of land to control openly and now covertly. And the
power lies with your Royal Family. Appearances do not tell the
real story. Buckingham Palace has a lid about to be removed
and what will come out will be beyond anyone's imagination.
You know the power of Washington. The power of London is
far greater. The London power has never lost control of
America. It merely hides the power and convinces the world
that the super power is America, when it is merely the child. If
you set the child free the parent will very rapidly be exposed
and conquered. You will be amazed at how quickly this will
happen from this moment.

"I have decided to withdraw from the battle for I cannot win.
The field is yours. The future is yours or rather; it belongs to
the energy you represent. I shall observe with enormous
interest what unfolds. I can see the future to an extent from
my dimensional plane of existence, but the future is changed
by thought. The future I saw led me to concede therefore the
future is changing very quickly, for my thought patterns are no
longer influencing that future. There is however an enormous
potential for chaos and an enormous vibrational and
emotional mess to clean up.

"You have my best thoughts as you seek to minimize the mess
and the chaos. We will meet again in better times when I have
balanced myself and you have completed your task."

This happened before the death of Diana, Princess of
Wales, and before the latest speculation about the Royal
Family came to the surface.

In the years that followed I remembered this incident and often read the above text to groups I worked with. People were often deeply touched when they heard these words. However it was only recently that I realized that the Ruby Red Reptile which had presented itself to Jacob and myself was the same energy as that which had spoken through David in Santa Barbara.

Only a short time ago this energy presented itself to Jacob and I again as we were having a telephone conversation. Jacob recognized it as the higher dimensional aspect of someone who is said to have been deeply involved in the reptilian agenda on this planet. I will refer to him here as Rex. In his third dimensional aspect Rex is a man who has been identified as having attended satanic rituals and as having abused children and other victims who were present. So it seems that this man Rex, the being that presented itself through David in Santa Barbara and the Ruby Red Reptile are in fact one. During the telephone conversation Jacob and I were having, the higher dimensional aspect of Rex told us the following, half in English and half in Danish. I had to tidy up the presentation:

> "I was responsible for the revolution of the reptiles long before they came to Earth. I was chosen to discover myself in my reptilian consciousness and then move the revolution in an upward going spiral. What you saw was right. (This refers to the fact that Jacob recognized the Ruby Red Reptile as the higher aspect of Rex.) I now work for the higher reptilian council and this gives me permission to connect (contact?) reptilians and call them to their home – to the Christ energy. I am pleased you recognized me and that you are not afraid of the darkness still vibrating in

my aura. I am pleased you at least saw the real self in this form.

"Tell your friend (i.e. Jacqueline) she is on the right track to finding the higher meaning of my presence. People working in this area usually only fill it with fears but we are a group that want to lift the reptiles to higher levels of consciousness and evolution. I come in peace and give the joy of this reptilian energy on Sirius. I am pleased my brother."

Jacob was then assured by his higher consciousness that all was well and was shown a reptilian base where those present were working for the light. He actually said there was very much light. He was shown that Rex had to come to the Earth plane in disguise in order to alter the course of things. I was on the other end of the telephone as this conversation was happening and my heart area became very warm and was strongly activated. I felt enormous love for the being presenting itself, very similar to the feeling in the car in Santa Barbara.

I remember the first time I asked Jacob about Rex. It was at a time when much was being written about his alleged activities and this was causing a lot of concern in many circles. It seemed as if there could be some truth in the reports of his having been involved in satanic abuse so I gave Jacob his name over the telephone and asked him to tune in to him. Jacob had never heard of him but tuned in and said that the only word that came was "trustworthy". I was quite surprised and asked again some weeks later. Again the reply came that this man was trustworthy. I hoped to be able to make some kind of contact with him, as I felt that being connected with this higher aspect of himself may be important in some way. When I wrote the second edition of this book I was able to tell that I had met Rex and had written an account of that meeting. Here it is...

Shortly after publishing the first edition of the book I went along to a meeting where Rex was to speak. My driver pulled up in the car park at the venue and went out of the car to find the entrance to the hall. As I was waiting a red car pulled up next to ours and I suddenly felt this car was important in some way. The door opened and Rex got out! He stood still, close to my window, and as I looked at him my stomach turned over. I found this interesting as my physical body usually gives me some very clear signals and I was tuning in to a very unpleasant energy. He stood by the window for some time and, staying with the physical sensations I felt inside, I just sat there repeating the Gayatri mantra.

When I went into the venue we were quite early so I went and sat alone in the refreshment bar. The next thing I knew was that Rex came and sat at the table next to me! There was no one else around. I felt an inner impulse to do some kind of energy work on the situation and suddenly realized that we were actually sitting in a triangular formation together with someone else: There was Rex, myself and a huge photograph of Queen Elizabeth of Britain! (Rex has quite a connection with the British Royal family.) I began to breathe into my heart and then create a circle of heart energy between Rex, Queen Elizabeth and myself. The energy became very powerful and in the midst of the circle I felt a strong presence and saw a ruby red color. As I continued breathing in this way I had the feeling I was to connect this ruby red presence with Rex. It felt as if they were actually one but that they were separated at that moment in time. As I registered this someone in the bar switched on the radio in the middle of Elton John's song, *Sacrifice*. A very appropriate title! However what amazed me most was the fact that the song came out over the air with the line, "two hearts living in two separate worlds"! I continued the energy work until it felt complete. Then I went and sat in the hall where, a few minutes later, I again found myself sitting next to Rex.

Later that day I heard him speak a couple of times. The first time I felt a powerful love vibration around him and seemed to feel the presence of the ruby red energy. In my heart I actually felt a great love for him. The second time he seemed more like an ordinary man giving an interesting lecture. I experienced him on three different levels that day: a lower "reptilian" level in the car, a higher dimensional level and an ordinary every day level. I later had an interesting talk with someone who also attended the day's event. He was a psychically sensitive man. As we talked about the lectures Rex had given he suddenly told me that he had heard Rex speak several times earlier but that something had been different this time. I asked what was different. He said that it was as if Rex was in connection with a higher aspect of himself that he hadn't been in contact with previously. I draw no conclusions here – just make of it what you will.

Looking back at what Jacob said over the telephone I remember he talked about giving the joy of the reptilian energy on Sirius. What this seems to tell me as I tune into it is that there are those of the reptilian race whose consciousness is connected with the energy of Sirius. It also suggests that the reptilian aspect of Rex has such a connection. One day I was reflecting on the subject of the reptiles and said to Jacob that I might include in this book a chapter entitled "Can Reptiles Get Enlightened?" It would be a chapter on the subject of the evolution of the reptiles towards higher consciousness. Jacob felt it was an idea that should be put out in some way and added:

> "Of course reptiles can get enlightened. We'd really be the bad guys if we said they couldn't – if we said they were completely evil!"

This is so true! This is a good time to remember the power of negative projections and the importance of neutrality. If people look at the information now coming to the surface and if they dwell on the "negative" it is more difficult for those involved to move beyond their present state. As I write a little later in this chapter, it can be difficult for someone to let go of a destructive pattern of behavior if he or she is always being confronted with someone else's negative response to this behavior.

To only focus on the lower level reptiles and their activities would be like someone writing a book about humans and only giving details of the lives of mass murderers. They could write about the murders and do psychological profiles on the murderers and then call the book, "Human Beings on Planet Earth." The information in the book may be correct but there would also be so much that was missing. It would give a totally imbalanced picture of human beings!

Right now I invite you to consider this fact: No matter how closed a person's heart becomes and no matter how negative or "evil" that person may appear to be, there is always the possibility of such a person waking up to the situation and leaving such a pathway behind. Let us also keep this in mind as we turn our attention to the British Royal Family.

I do not intend to repeat all the information given out by researchers on the secrets of the Royal Family. As I said at the start, this book has been written to supplement other research and to give a different perspective on certain issues. Anyone who has read the research done by people such as Jan van Helsing, David Icke and Scott Thompson[2] will know that those of the House of Windsor and other European Royals are accused of being involved in some very questionable dealings. Suffice it to say that they seem to have been involved in some very dark matters for many centuries. However it must be remembered that families such as the Windsors are not at the heart of the manipulation – not what is often referred to as "top of the pyramid". Even though they are close to the top, they are still being used in some way. Here are a few examples of things uncovered by different researchers.

In his very fine book, *Secret Societies and Their Power in the 20th Century*, Jan van Helsing quotes a passage from an article entitled "The Queen and Narcotics". The article was written in the September 8, 1993 edition of *Neue Solidaritat*. Here is a brief passage from the article:

> "From original documents the *Leopard*[3] proved that Queen Victoria and her entourage, often the Churchill and Rothschild

---

[2] See for example: *Secret Societies And Their Power In The 20th Century* by Jan van Helsing. ...*And The Truth Shall Set You Free* by David Icke, *The Nazi Roots Of The House Of Windsor* and *The Ultimate Inside Intruder Is The Queen* both by Scott Thompson

---

[3] A Scottish magazine

families, had standing orders for sizeable quantities of cocaine, heroine and other narcotics with a highland pharmacy. The *Times* averred the same. It said: "Queen Victoria, the monarch with the severe mien, well-known for her 'We are not amused' seems to have ordered enough cocaine and heroin for her Balmoral estate in Scotland to keep a whole Highland valley 'high'. The papers of the pharmacy 'show that the Royals and their guests were regularly supplied with considerable amounts of cocaine and heroin solutions'."

It is said to be quite common knowledge that the Windsors are involved in the narcotics trade, but what is perhaps not so well known is the real nature of the World Wide Fund For Nature (WWF) set up by Prince Philip and Prince Bernhard of the Netherlands. In his book, *The Biggest Secret*, David Icke claims that the WWF was not set up to protect endangered species of animals. He says:

"The WWF was created for very different reasons. It is a vehicle for controlling wildlife parks in Africa and elsewhere in which terrorist groups and mercenaries can gather, train and cross borders to bring genocide to places like Rwanda and Burundi. The WWF coordinates and funds the systematic slaughter of people and animals and has made a fortune from the illegal trade in ivory it was supposed to be trying to stop. Much of this is being paid for by donations from the public who think they are supporting wildlife and collected by fund-raisers in the towns and cities who believe the same."

Then follows a passage about the big game hunter, Ian Parker, who was commissioned to write a report on the illegal trade in elephant tusks and rhino horns. Sir Peter

Scott, a well-known conservationist, commissioned the report. I quote again from *The Biggest Secret*:

> "Parker produced evidence that the family of the Kenyan President, Jomo Kenyatta, was at the centre of this trade. He also named Kenya's most prominent 'conservationists' as the poachers. Within hours of handing his report to Scott, Parker was arrested by Kenyan Special Branch, beaten for three days, and told if he did not shut up his wife would be killed.[4] Parker's report was never published by Scott and at around the same time Prince Bernhard, as WWF International President, awarded Kenyatta the 'Order of the Golden Ark' for saving the rhino!"

As part of the confirmation that the Royal Family is involved in the devious plots of the intelligence agencies, David Icke gives an account of an incident reported by Colonel David Sterling, founder of the SAS. Sterling told the following story to the authors of the book *Who Killed Diana?* He told them that in late 1974 or early 1975 he attended a dinner hosted by a senior member of the monarchy. (In *The Biggest Secret* it is suggested that this was Prince Philip.) David gives the following account:

> "Prince Charles' uncle, Lord Mountbatten, was there along with ten representatives of British Intelligence including the heads of MI5 and MI6. They were there in an unofficial capacity and Stirling pointed out that all military officers swore allegiance to the Queen and regarded her as the ultimate authority, more important than the elected

---

[4] *The Oligarch's Real game Is Killing Animals And Killing People* by Allen Douglas

governments. The meeting was called to discuss the state of the country and the need for intervention in political affairs. The use of force was on the agenda, he said. Stirling told the meeting of his involvement in an operation to create a coup d'etat on Libya and at the time he was the leader of an organisation called GB75 which was designed to take over public services in times of crisis. John Mitchell, the chairman of the shipping company, Cunard, also confirmed that he had been approached to take part in a coup because they wanted his ships. One of the orchestrators was Sir Basil Smallpiece, financial advisor to the Queen. Mitchell said:

"They asked me to take part in a coup. They said it would involve the army. They implied it had the highest backing... I went out of there in a state of shock."

David Icke actually says that the Windsors must know that time is running out for them and that "the game is up". He suggests they may abdicate and move to the United States. Looking at the horoscope of Queen Elizabeth ll, I'd say that was very possible. There are certainly some sweeping changes on the way. Let's take a look at her astrological chart.

In her birth chart she has quite a tense yet dynamic combination of planets in what is called a T square configuration. At the midpoint of the T square she has the planet Saturn right next to the mid heaven in Scorpio. We can see here that the image presented to the world is an image of respectability. It is also that of an authoritarian figure, quite controlled and serious. Saturn's placement here in Scorpio also suggests a part to be played where lessons will be learned in connection with the proper use of power.

In very challenging aspects to the Scorpio combination we have Mars and Jupiter together in Aquarius and Neptune in Leo. The planets in the signs of Aquarius and Leo also oppose each other.

All aspects in a chart have a higher potential, no matter how challenging. So the above combination can show someone who is a real crusader, fighting for equality and freedom. It can be a real "systems buster" aspect – a voice of change fighting totally unselfishly for what it believes in. This person could be totally dedicated, although a bit over zealous and could sometimes be misguided and not able to distinguish between visions for the future and what is possible right here and now. That is one level of interpretation – there are others. This aspect could also show deceitful and underhanded actions and could denote someone who was involved in very shady activities connected with occult practices and with narcotics. There could also be issues connected with morality, sound judgement and integrity. It could be difficult for this person to live her deepest truth.

Of course a birth horoscope doesn't just stand still. The planets constantly activate it as they move around in the heavens. These movements are called "transits". At this very moment the planet Uranus is about to begin a two year long activation of the T square in the Queen's horoscope. I often call Uranus the alarm clock of the zodiac. It is "the awakener" and usually awakens people through unexpected and quite shocking events. It can be a very sudden disruptive force which, once unleashed, seems to blow through the life of the person concerned stripping him or her of illusions, limiting structures and out worn patterns of behavior. As with all transits of the outer transpersonal planets it is not possible to stay in control of events. It is certainly not advisable to try – the keyword is "let go".

At the same time as this is happening, the planet Pluto is beginning to transit Venus in the Queen's chart in quite a challenging way. The main keywords for Pluto are death, destruction of the old and consequent rebirth. Venus is traditionally known as the planet of love, beauty and harmony. It "rules" the fourth house in this chart – the house connected with the home, family, roots and traditions. So there are definitely going to be changes and very often these are forced changes with Pluto in this particular aspect. Pluto is often seen as the hand of fate that reminds us nothing lasts forever, and if we can totally embrace Pluto we can really live with detachment. We can actually already see Pluto at work here. On the evening of June 3rd 2000 the Queen attended the same function as Camilla Parker-Bowles, Prince Charles' partner. Up until that point it is said that the Queen refused such a meeting. Venus also rules what we appreciate and being able to appreciate other people's values and life styles. Ruling the 4th house of her chart it now brings up family issues – Prince Charles' wish to have the woman he has chosen acknowledged by his mother. Pluto brings death to an old outworn pattern of behavior and ultimately can release a greater level of love and respect in Queen Elizabeth.

Exactly what all of these different aspects working together will mean for the Queen of England I cannot say as Uranus also brings the unexpected. However I would say that things which have been hidden cannot stay hidden for much longer and there will certainly be some element of shock, surprise and change in her life in the time ahead. As Jacob said some time ago, the British Royal Family only exists because people look up to them. In the time ahead I'd say it is not about looking down on them, it's about seeing right through the game and the pretence and deciding it is over.

Since I wrote the first edition of this book the Queen has of course experienced the death of her sister, Princess Margaret and her mother, the Queen Mother. They died within a short time of each other. Here we see the energies of both Pluto and Uranus – death and surprise or shock. Uranus also brings potential freedom and perhaps the Queen will now be free to make more enlightened changes than she could have made had the Queen Mother still been alive.

Let us now go off in a different direction – there are many threads I need to pull together in this chapter. What follows now is taken from a meeting Jacob and I had in a different café in Copenhagen in March 1999, just before I held the follow-up days to David's speaking tour in England. Again I have translated from Danish. Jacob says:

> "The reptiles are allowed to be here on equal terms with other races – also to develop free will. Remember that humans also kill in this dimension just as beings in other dimensions also perform rituals and sacrifice other beings. Reptiles also fight each other and want power – they are also limited. They live in a certain frequency pocket. There are also reptiles in the inner earth – physical reptiles – but they don't mix with us. Reptiles are in kindergarten here – a quick development is possible because of the heavy vibrations.
>
> "Long ago the Star People came – some central consciousnesses up at the Central Sun were sent out through

the different dimensions. Some received the 'Ruby Red Heart'[5] on Alfa Orega. This shows a mission concerned with teaching others acceptance of and love for everything created. Some of these great star consciousnesses, after stepping down their vibrations, incarnated in the reptilian frequency. They received reptilian genes and entered into the reptilian evolution. Just as great beings can fall in our system, so too in the reptilian system, and some ended up in satanic type rituals. Some clairvoyants see this and imagine it's all happening on the physical plane.

"For example, the Queen Mother[6] could be from Kuska and could be a great solar angel there. She could have light bodies many different places – with the reptiles, ETs, humans etc. Perhaps Arizona Wilder imagines that the light body she sees with the reptiles is physical. Often these races still sacrifice etc. and the highly developed souls do this because it needs to be done with love. They have a part to play and although a shell of anger and aggression surrounds them, behind this shell shines this love. This means that those who are sacrificed are not lost forever.

One reason why these people incarnate as Kings, Presidents etc. is that a high energy is needed. These posts have always been

---

[5] As I write this I remember being told years ago that I had much ruby red color in my energy field. Jacob later described this color as unconditional love that was given freely to many. He talked about a mother with her first new-born baby being totally absorbed in the baby and giving it all her love and attention. This has its own beauty. However if a mother has a new born baby and 12 other children she has to be able to give out her love in a different way so it is available for all 13 children! She may need to be more detached and disciplined but the love is still there. He actually said that the ruby red colour represented a very high love frequency.

[6] With regards to the late Queen Mother let us not be naïve here about the part she played in this dimension – I know it was far from angelic!

filled by highly developed souls. These posts eventually have to be given over to humans but this cannot be done as long as humans still kill and sacrifice. When looking at the so-called "conspiracy" it is very important that people do not judge. If people can remain neutral these hidden things will begin to reveal themselves. It is important not to go into fear, not to want to "reveal" things for the sake of it and it is also important to be able to embrace the knowledge that these things are happening. On one level it really is OK that these things are happening. One reason we don't exist side by side with other dimensions is that if we did we would judge what was happening there. When the great star souls are at war with each other – and remember that the planet has made itself available for this – the war can only continue if we choose sides."

I would just like to come in her and stress once more how important this last message is. I know I have said the same thing many times now, but cannot stress it enough and have very good reasons for returning to this point so often. I'll put it this way – if a great war suddenly seems to happen in the heavens or on the physical plane let's remember the slogan I first saw written on a banner so many years ago in the musical *Hair*:

"What if they had a war and nobody came!"

So, back to Jacob's message:

"Yes – Rockefeller controls a lot, but if we judge it or push it away we give it the emotional energy it feeds off. The great Star Souls didn't live off emotional energy to start with but, because of the genes they've put into the planet and the different races, they now live off emotional energy. Therefore, as you yourself so often say Jacqueline, enlightenment is the most important thing to focus on. We have to go beyond emotional energy. Emotional energy creates, but if it is together with "ego" – and this applies to all races – it has to be purified and transformed. Creative energy is intelligence, love and fire – these three elements.

"Let's take the example of Edward Heath.[7] An ordinary person experiences the veils opening – and many are experiencing this today. If that person goes into panic it can not bring in the light and the veil will close. Try to keep a door open and manifest an energy that will lift those who do such things.

"The British Royals are not Satanists on the physical plane, but they were further back in time. They suffer much – there is much pain in their hearts and therefore they are cold. It is only possible to hold such a post if there is a strong love vibration. The Windsors are a family from way back who have fought other families and gone through a kind of development where they had to build a shell to keep their power. But this line is in the process of transformation. Look more to the politicians – here we have satanic rituals on the physical plane. If someone has great power they either have it because of great love or great ego!

"I remember Marina[8] telling that she saw the energy of the Christ Consciousness around Queen Elizabeth at the time of her coronation. There is just as much dark as light. She has to

---

[7] See chapter 5

[8] Marina is a Danish woman Jacob and I know. She also has exceptional psychic gifts

take part in the things that happen in the dimension she chooses to incarnate in. Diana brought in light because she agreed to the role – she also agreed to die in a ritualistic murder."

There is something I have often said which is similar to part of what Jacob is saying here: anyone with a major role in the drama now being played out on this planet is a highly developed soul, even if the role being played seems to be a "dark" one. Look at the high degree of discipline, detachment and self sacrifice needed to fulfil the demands of such a role. A highly developed soul who has closed down part of the heart chakra and moved deeply into the dark can change at any moment. I talked about this in *The Last Waltz* and actually said at some point:

"A lot of loving acceptance is needed when a person is ready to let go of the struggle, and when the person concerned lets go much power is released – power for transformation. A great leap in consciousness takes place. I feel that many of those at the peak of the manipulation are struggling now and that loving hands held out to them could work miracles"
…and a little later… "an open heart can always extend a hand to other aspects of the oneness it meets along the way."

I do feel it is important to be able to embrace whatever is happening with detachment. If we judge and condemn the players in this drama we actually help to keep them locked in the roles they are playing. Let's really bring this idea down to earth here. You probably know what it can be like in a relationship when one person keeps on commenting about a certain behavior pattern of the other. Imagine, for example, someone who seems to have an addiction to watching television always being confronted with the following by his or her partner: "Why do you always close down when I bring up the subject of you watching television? You are a television addict and need to be able to talk about it. You should be able to switch the thing off for my sake. You need some therapy. I'm beginning to feel it's my fault you can't open up…" and so on.

Such a person can end up really stuck. However, the same person can talk with someone who is not involved emotionally – a therapist perhaps – who can address the issue without having any judgement on it. If there is total acceptance the person with the "problem" can suddenly also accept himself totally. "Miracles" can happen in such situations as limiting patterns of behavior are left behind and the person concerned moves up to a new level of experience.

Jacob has stated many times that the Windsors have said "yes" to change and that they said this yes when they lowered the flag in respect to Diana. He said they have opened up on some level and agreed to be lifted. He does not say this in a naîve manner, pretending that they are all light and love and nothing else! He says there is still much darkness, but that there is the intention to leave this behind and say yes to the enlightened reptilian energy. I also feel this is the case. Not so long ago I spoke with a young guy from South Africa who often has visionary dreams. He had dreamed that the Queen of England had approached him wanting to know how to begin her transformation process. In the dream she seemed "genuinely open" to learning how to become more positive and to break out of the control being forced upon her. I don't want to place too much emphasis on this dream, as it could, of course, be an aspect of his own feminine side we see here. There are many ways to look at it. However, because of who he is, I just felt it was worth mentioning.

Earlier on in this chapter I wrote about the fact that Jacob said certain clairvoyants could see things that were taking place in light bodies in different dimensions, and then imagine it was happening down here on the physical plane. I'd like to say a little more about this and to do so I go back to a couple of incidents which took place in New Zealand at the beginning of 1999.

Someone who had been visiting me was just about to leave when she said that she'd been thinking how strange it was that Einstein invented or worked on a time machine and today, so many years later, we don't really hear any more about time machines. I remember her saying that things like that don't just disappear. Shortly after she left the phone rang and it was someone I knew quite well in England who had just arrived in New Zealand. She started telling me about someone in England who had contacted her and told her about strange happenings at Sandringham – one of the residences of the British Royal Family. She had been given information about some of the Royals coming to Sandringham and going somewhere within the house and just disappearing. She was told that some of them, Prince Charles included, just disappeared for days on end and then appeared again.

Some days later I was talking with a contact who can see inter-dimensionally. Part of what was said I've already written, but I repeat it again here in a little more detail. I did not mention the above conversations to my contact, but simply told of Arizona Wilder's accounts with regards to the

Royals being shape-shifting reptiles involved in human sacrifice. The following reply was given with a shudder:

> "Ugh – when I go in to take a look at what's happening it's pretty awful! It's as if they are doing such things, but it's not here. You can walk into their house and they're not there, but they are 'there'. They go to their place, do what they do and come back."

I then asked the question, "They come back fortified in their "reptilianness" you mean?" The answer was:

> "Yes. They have to do it 'cos everything needs a battery and that's their battery. Arizona Wilder probably sees it and thinks it's happening down here."

There is one thing I have wondered about: If the Queen is a shape-shifting reptile and is tearing babies apart at satanic rituals, why does she have such a wonderful contact with her animals? Why don't the animals pick up on this energy and show fear? We are told that one of the reasons Arizona Wilder is programmed to perform rituals for Illuminati families is that they cannot perform the rituals themselves because they do not have much psychic energy. Such energies are closed down in them as they are cold emotionally.

From the British *Daily Mail* newspaper I collected a series of ten magazines entitled "A Century of Royals". Each magazine focused on a different member of the family or topic. Of course I don't believe everything I read in newspapers, but I just wanted to read something written from a different perspective and to study the photographs.

The seventh edition, entitled "If only they could talk", focused on pets and other animals belonging to the Royal Family. There are many photographs of the Royals and the animals and on page 2 we read about the gun dogs from the Sandringham kennels and are told:

> "All are working dogs, many trained by the Queen herself, who, as our delightful picture indicates, seems to share an extraordinary psychic link with animals. Before they can possibly know her car has arrived at the gates, there is always an outbreak of excited barking."

Someone I questioned about this said that the animals were probably micro-chipped and controlled to behave in such a way. This could, of course, be true but it didn't feel right to me. However I rang a woman who is an expert on dogs and runs dog kennels. She doesn't know me or my work but was willing to answer a few questions. I asked her how a dog would behave if it had a master or mistress who was really "evil". I told her I did not mean that the dog itself was mistreated but that very evil deeds, such as torture and murder, were done to others. I said I wondered if the dog would react in any way. The kennel owner told me that the dog would definitely pick such things up and although it would probably still be obedient it wouldn't be affectionate. She did say that different breeds have different temperaments and when I especially asked about Corgies she said that they could probably turn "quite nasty" under such circumstances.

Another thing that struck me as I read this series and looked at the photographs was how beautiful the Queen looked as a very young woman, especially before her

Coronation. Back in 1997 I worked with a group of people up at Findhorn in Scotland and asked them to psychically tune in to the Coronation ceremony and the crown placed on the head of the monarch during the ceremony. Some of those present, myself included, felt there was something in the ceremony that linked the new King or Queen with the malevolent agenda of manipulation on this planet. I would also suggest that one of the jewels in the crown is actually coded with this agenda. I am also quite sure that Queen Elizabeth is fully aware of what she is doing and what the rest of the Royals are up to. I make no judgement here, just an observation. I feel this part of the game is almost over.

A few weeks after I had written this chapter I had a powerful connection with Sirius and was actually told that Queen Elizabeth has a light body on Sirius. I have checked this with a couple of reliable sources and they confirmed it was so.

I am not afraid to look at things as they really are and at the same time I feel we must perhaps be careful not to see absolutely everything as a sign of people being Satanists, reptiles and so on. For example many ask how Prince Charles can be a conservationist and still go fox hunting. It is almost as if this is proof of the fact that he is a Satanist. I'm not saying he is or he isn't, yet I know many people who say they love animals and abhor cruelty to animals and yet they are still meat eaters. I also suddenly remember a young guy for whom I recently did a horoscope reading. He's an old soul and really awake spiritually. However he suddenly admitted to getting a real buzz from street fighting and seemed quite surprised that this was so. He had Mars and Uranus together in the twelfth house of his chart and this is quite an explosive combination of energies. The twelfth house is connected with unconscious urges that can take people by surprise, and it is also connected with behavior patterns that can seem to work against or sabotage the conscious identity. There can be an aggressive, violent streak in the astrological combination mentioned here, but this is part of this person's make-up and, as he is conscious of it, he doesn't need to act it out in a destructive way. All sides of the psyche need to be acknowledged and all sides need some form of outlet for their energies.

Prince Charles has aspects in his horoscope that could easily manifest as a love for blood sports. At the same time there are aspects which suggest a real love for the earth and an interest in conservation. There is a refined sense of beauty, artistic talent and a capacity for unconditional love. I recently heard a recording of a talk on sustainable development given by Prince Charles as part of the Reith Lectures. It was a powerful and gentle presentation that acknowledged man's stewardship for the Earth and the importance of listening to and following the wisdom of the heart. Many people's horoscopes show seemingly opposite traits within the same psyche, and allowing each part to fulfil its most enlightened potential is something an understanding of astrological archetypes can support.

There is one final thread I would like to introduce into this chapter. January 1999 I was in Byron Bay, Australia and one day found myself walking into a kind of New Age shop and asking for a Tarot reading with a woman who worked there. I had never met her or seen the shop before, but something just pulled me in. This was not something I would normally do. It was only a couple of months after the Sedona event and David Icke was putting out very strong messages about satanic rituals attended by shape-shifting

Royals. I wanted a reading from someone who knew nothing about me, David or the strange things that seemed to be happening in the world. That was exactly what I got. The woman was wonderful – very clear and intuitive. In the beginning she thought I had just come in for a personal reading, but very soon realized this was not the case. At the end of the reading she just seemed to want to do something for me. I was moving to another guesthouse and she carried my luggage out for me and put me in a taxi. She was saying things like, "Where have I been all this time? I had no idea such things were going on!"

During the reading she quickly picked up on goings on within politics and the Royal Family and at one point during the reading she said:

> "There is so much awful darkness and it's been going on for years, yet this darkness can never win. It's on all levels – all levels of the hierarchy. I'm finding it really shocking! The whole thing has to be uncovered before the new young Royals come into power – especially William and Harry. It has to be changed because they are such little light beings – they couldn't enter into such darkness. All of this is happening now for the benefit of the children."

She also picked up on misinformation being given to David, but said that in the end "the shit will hit the fan" and justice will be done.

So, how do I sum up this chapter? I don't want to draw too many conclusions and pretend to know exactly what's going on and who's doing what. I can say, however that the Royals are probably giving a performance which, once revealed, is going to shock many people. This is fine – great awakenings can happen when people are shocked out of their sleep. In the British National anthem, *God Save the Queen* there is the line,

> "Send her victorious, happy and glorious…"

I also wish this for the Queen and for all of the Royals. May this be a true victory of the heart – the heart that has responded to the spiritual call of the times and said yes to change. May you move through this change quickly, especially for the sake of the young ones, as they do not deserve to inherit such darkness. I hope you can feel the support of those of us who have gone beyond judgement as we welcome home all aspects of the one consciousness we call life.

11

A guiding hand from Sirius

"Our birth is but a sleep and a forgetting:
The soul that rises with us, our life's star
Hath had elsewhere its setting,
And cometh from afar;
Not in entire forgetfulness,
And not in utter nakedness,
But trailing clouds of glory do we come
From God, who is our home."

Wordsworth

It is time to start remembering on Planet Earth and it is encouraging to see that much suppressed and forgotten information about advanced civilizations from the past is now coming to the surface. One such civilization is Sirius, sometimes described as the Father aspect of Planet Earth. Sirius, a very highly developed civilization, is found in the constellation of Canis Major and is about 8.7 light years away from Earth. In his book, *The Sirius Mystery*, Robert Temple provides information about the Dogon tribe who are found near Timbuktu in Mali, West Africa. Apparently this tribe has had information for over 700 years that scientists on Earth have only had for about 30 years. The elders of the tribe kept this information safe through their ancient oral tradition and in the villages children learned about their Sirian ancestors. Temple's book was based on the research of two French anthropologists, Marcel Griaule and Germaine Dieterlau who visited the Dogon people between 1946 and 1950.

These people shared their secrets with the anthropologists. They told them much about Sirius, the brightest star in our sky, and also said that a very small star moved around Sirius. They knew that this small star was very old, that it was made of the heaviest matter known to us and they also had precise details of the nature of the star's rotation. These details were confirmed by scientists in the seventies and the small star was named Sirius B. The original Sirius then became known as Sirius A. It is interesting that Robert Temple's book was released in 1977, the same year as the planetary body Chiron was sighted. Chiron is said to have attributes very similar to those of Sirius B, which include very powerful healing properties. Chiron and Sirius B both take 50 years to orbit Earth and Sirius A respectively.[1]

The tribal elders told researchers visiting the Dogon people how they had obtained such knowledge. They told about a flying saucer that landed carrying dolphin-like beings who made a hole in the ground and filled it with water. It is said they jumped into the water and came to talk to the Dogon people. Apparently they said they were from Sirius and gave them much information and facts about Sirius and also about other planets unknown to man at that point in time. They gave very precise information about Uranus and Neptune – information that was actually confirmed when these two planets were "discovered" hundreds of years later!

---

[1] Read more in The Pleiadian Agenda, Barbara Hand Clow – Appendix D

In the ancient Hopi mythology we can read of 3 worlds which have already passed out of existence. The Hopis say that in the first world there were four types of people: red, yellow, white and black. There were also the "Star People" – star beings who were not human. They were said to have come from Sirius and Orion and are also found in the myths of the Maya, the ancient Egyptians and, of course, the Dogon tribe mentioned here.

According to some sources the Sirians have had a strong interest in Planet Earth since the creation of Homo sapiens, and it is said that the Sirians helped the Anunnaki – Nephilim from Nibiru to create humans. I don't know if this is accurate or not, but it is well accepted that the Sirians have been very involved with our planet in the past and that they were especially involved with the Egyptians and the Mayans. I also know that the Sirian energy is still helping to inspire the consciousness on this planet and lift it to a higher vibration. When I met Credo Mutwa in South Africa he said that the reptilian "Chitauri" were actually afraid of humans. He said they wanted to keep us away from space and from Sirius, our original home.

It also seems the Pleiadians and the Sirians have now formed an alliance and are working together to help us through the times ahead – working to help but not to interfere. Both the Sirians and the Pleiadians seem to agree that it is time to end Anunnaki suppression of consciousness on Earth. I also understand that the Sirians are trying out ways of getting the Anunnaki to feel instead of think and yet of course they also acknowledge the roles the people of Earth and the Anunnaki have played out together. There is a teaching here for any who still judge the drama being played out. Seen from a more enlightened level of consciousness, which the Sirians have, everything is fine. It is also fine to feel and follow the impulse to make changes.

I have a very strong Sirian connection myself which, amongst other things, reminds me of the dolphin energy of joy and celebration, so I'll throw in a story here – take it as you wish. Several years ago I was speaking to someone who sees the personification of energies from other dimensions and she was describing the differences between beings from Sirius and Andromeda. She said the Sirians often appeared to her in flimsy, see-through garments and that they were very light and flowing in their energy. Those from Andromeda she described as more "efficient". I remember her saying she often saw them dressed in what looked like jumpsuits and that they seemed to be a more organized type.

Some time after I talked with this woman I was invited to hold an evening talk in Odense, Denmark, and the theme for the evening was going to be interplanetary co-operation and the initiation of Planet Earth. I would be focusing on Sirius and also bringing in a little about Andromeda, this being my place of origin after individuation. It was a beautiful summer evening and, as I was walking across the lawn to the venue, I suddenly became aware of what I was wearing. The evening sun was still strong and I realized that as it shone on me my new dress was totally transparent – you could see straight through it! I also became aware of the smart leather briefcase I was carrying containing papers and music for the evening – very efficiently organized. What a contrast! Then I remembered the Sirians and the Andromedans and felt in that moment that I embodied both energies. I knew both were very strong in me and that they always worked well together and complemented each other.

Here's one other story that might be of interest. Although Sirius is often called the Dog Star it is said that cats carry the star consciousness of Sirius and birds that of the Pleiades.[2] I had a very special cat for almost 15 years. Her name was Tara. At the beginning of 1999 the time came for her to leave the Earth plane and of course I was very sad. Some months later I showed her photograph to the Shaman from New Zealand I wrote about in an earlier chapter. She contacted Tara and told me she had taken the form of a bird. She was surprised, but said that it seemed Tara had known she could fly and wanted to experience flying in a physical form. I was happy to hear this as I have also always known I can fly. I often feel her very close to me and like the idea of her own little Sirian – Pleiadian alliance!

During a powerful line up of planets in the sign of Taurus I was in Glastonbury, England, where I "time-traveled" under hypnosis. I went easily into a very deep state and immediately slipped through a golden silk curtain to the Pyramids of Egypt around 10,700BC and found myself in a former incarnation which was very definitely Sirian inspired. (Egypt was built on Sirian archetypes and the Pyramids were constructed on sacred Sirian geometry.) This was not at all what I had expected. I was actually looking for a key to help with something I was researching and had a feeling I knew where I was going to find it. I had not expected Egypt or Sirius!

The strength of the golden sun in the sky was immense. The sands of the desert seemed golden – everything was shining and shimmering and I myself seemed to be semi physical – semi etheric. I was reminded of the importance of

---

[2] According to *The Pleiadian Agenda* cats live the energy of Sirius, birds the Pleiades, bears the Andromeda Galaxy and lizards that of Draco

sound and vibration as a tool for lifting consciousness on the planet. I remembered my name as being "Nada" and realized later that this means "sound" in the Sanskrit language. As I lay there under hypnosis the title of a movie kept coming to me. I could remember the title in Danish, "Tilvaerelsens Ulidelige Lethed". In English I believe it is something like, *The Unbearable Lightness of Being*. It starred Daniel Day Lewis, Juliette Binoche and Lena Olin. I always loved the title of that movie and felt the words symbolized a way of being we were to rediscover in our more cosmic future. The main direction of my work I call "Celebration as a Pathway to Enlightenment". I know this pathway embodies, amongst other things, the energy of Sirius. It combines detached, unconditional love, joy, lightness and celebration. Sirius is the archetype of the alchemist and my work is about alchemy. The alchemy of the heart brings the freedom to follow energy pathways through life and it brings the freedom to follow the song of the flow of life, moving beyond all conditionings. Somewhere I came across a quotation from the Sirian Codice of Understanding:

> "…It is best to understand the Universe and its song, for its harmony plays your inner truth."

I also feel the Pleiadian influence in the music, dancing and celebration of the heart combined with the "systems buster" energy that is also a large part of this work. During the connection with Sirius I was reminded of an evening I'd held some years ago in Aalborg, Denmark – an evening on Sirius. After the presentation I had lain awake most of the night immersed in a high vibrational golden – white energy.

Sirius is a sixth dimensional energy and gives the ability to be in tune with sacred geometry. As I write this it reminds me that I often experience Sirius as having the blueprints of a higher vibrational potential of whatever is happening on Earth. Great inspiration comes just by "hanging out" in the Sirian energy. Many years ago, tuning in to my Sirian lightbody, I experienced myself doing a similar kind of energy work that I often do here on Earth using music and special energy formations of people. It was much lighter and more cosmic up there, but I knew that the inspiration for the work on this plane came from the higher dimensional light body.

In an earlier chapter I mentioned the work of Sheldon Nidle, co-author of *You Are Becoming a Galactic Human*. Sheldon had apparently been contacted by the Sirians as a very young boy and is said to be working closely with them today. He had some interesting things to say about responsibility for the evolution of Earth that I'd like to tell about here. Way back in time, guardianship of Planet Earth was given to three different groups; one group being what we today call the "Spiritual Hierarchy" of the planet. (I'd just like to say here that what I understand by this is the Master consciousness which has gone before us and which, as a higher collective energy field, now guides and inspires this planet to higher levels of consciousness. I do not mean all these "ascended masters" currently being channeled by New Agers.) The second group was the cetaceans – the dolphins and whales – and we can certainly see them playing a role in opening people's hearts and minds and healing them on a very deep level. Anyone who has been in contact with dolphins will confirm they carry a very high energy. The third group was us – I'd say an important reminder of our responsibility for this planet.

When Sheldon Nidle's book came out in 1995 it caused quite a stir because of information it contained about Earth's dramatic entry into the "Photon Belt" which was predicted to take place before the end of 1996. It was said that on entry there would be three days of total darkness, freezing temperatures, opening up of all psychic abilities and much more! There would be mass landings by the Sirians who would do what needed to be done to get us safely through this period, and this would include putting us in a holographic bubble at some point and moving us many light years closer to Sirius. If anything this book certainly got many people "up out of the sofa" as we say in Danish!

For readers who have not heard of the Photon Belt here is a brief description. Let us first remember that Earth is a planet orbiting a Pleiadian star. Photon simply means light and the Photon Belt, which is 2,000 years wide, is a doughnut shaped belt or band of high vibrational light which circles Alcyone, the brightest star in the constellation of the Pleiades. The Sun in our Solar System takes about 25,000 – 26,000 years to circle Alcyone and in this way we experience 2,000 years in the Photon Belt every 11,000 – 12,000 years. Being immersed in such an enlightened energy field brings the possibility of real enlightenment. However it can also cause a great shake-up and much turmoil as whatever is not functioning at a high vibrational level is either provoked and transformed or destroyed. This is how I see the effect of coming into contact with the Photon Belt.

As I understand it, we are already to some degree in the energies of the Photon Belt as different planets in our Solar System enter at different points in time. Some enter briefly and come out again until gradually the whole system is immersed in this energy. I'd say that as each planet enters the Photon Belt, whatever aspect of life and consciousness that planet represents will be subjected to a shake-up and a lift! It is said by some that Earth's orbit will be fully in the belt in 2013. This makes some sense to me and also suggests that this is the time where all beings still on Planet Earth will understand what the "Age of Aquarius" is really about. You probably know that Aquarius represents enlightenment and the realization of God in man. By "God in man" I mean in every man and not just in one or in a few chosen ones. I also find it interesting that Barbara Hand Clow[3] gives the Earth's point of entry into the Photon Belt as 0 degrees Libra. (Interesting because of the energy of 0 degrees Libra and also because it is the position of the Sun in my own horoscope!) The Sabien symbol[4] given for this degree of Libra is as follows:

> "In a collection of perfect specimens of many biological forms, a butterfly displays the beauty of its wings, its body impaled by a fine dart."

(Interesting to note that butterflies as well as birds are associated with the Pleiades.) The keynote given for this symbol is:

> "The immortal archetypal reality that a perfect and dedicated life reveals."

The writer then goes on to explain this degree in the following way:

---

[3] *The Pleiadian Agenda*, page 28

[4] *The Pleiadian Agenda*, page 257

> "The impaled butterfly is preserved by a dart which 'fixes' it in perfection for a whole cycle i.e. makes an archetype of it. By thus escaping the normal process of dying and decay, the butterfly form (the perfection) is kept."

What comes to me on reading this is initiation – merging with a higher level of consciousness or with the blueprint for this incarnation. Hence we have "perfection" or realizing the highest aspect available in this particular cycle. So I see the possibility of planetary initiation or enlightenment.

Sheldon Nidle actually says that "Supreme Creator" has arranged for us to be in a holographic bubble of protection instead of putting us into the Void. He says that the bubble will thrust us out of the Photon Belt and into the 5th Dimension to a position 3 light years away from Sirius. This should happen before 2013. We could look at this symbolically and say that higher dimensional energies are working to protect and keep people on Earth stable as the energies intensify. We, the guardians, are here to find creative ways of "building bridges", creating a more enlightened society and thereby helping people become accustomed to a higher energy field. I feel much of this work could be completed by the end of 2012 – the date for the end of the Mayan Calendar. You can read more about this in the next chapter.

I don't want to make further comments on the predictions Sheldon Nidle made at that time or speculate over what happened to him after the release of the book. You can re-read the comments made in chapter 4 of this book. However, I would like to share some of the information he shared about Sirius that I find plausible and useful. So here it is.

He says that Sirian influence on Earth began about 2,000,000BC in the colonies of Hyperborea and later in Lemuria – very beautiful and harmonic civilizations. After Atlantis destroyed Lemuria around 11,000 years ago, Sirius no longer influenced Earth in the same way as we came more under the Pleiadian influence. Dates given here are, of course, quite flexible. (Barbara Hand Clow also suggests that the Sirian connection with Egypt was severed at this time as the ancient wisdom fell into the hands of the Hebrew priests and the infiltration and perversion of the mystery school teachings began. It seems these priests actually got hold of energies from Nibiru and not Sirius and in this way brought the Nibiruan conflict onto the earth plane. This is the conflict we are still attempting to solve today. It manifests as religious fundamentalism as opposed to true pathways to spiritual enlightenment.)

In 1972 Sirius intervened in order to prevent Earth being wiped out by an explosion on the Sun. There were actually brief newspaper reports about this explosion and then nothing more was said about it. Towards the end of 1992 Sirius and the Pleiadians together began influencing us through a joint alliance they formed to help us break free of Anunnaki control and the low vibrational net of conditioning which has grown around Earth. I have also read that it is the Sirians who are our main guides when Earth is traveling outside of the Photon Belt and the Pleiadians guide us when we travel through it. It makes sense to me that both are working together during this changeover period. The Sirian and Pleiadian alliance is an interesting one as the Pleiadian energy is feminine – the archetypal goddess energy – and Sirius is masculine – the archetype of the alchemist. The Sirians are also said to release the knowledge we need to remember and the Pleiadians help to open up the hearts of humanity. The planetary initiation we are moving towards on Earth demands the perfect balance of masculine and feminine energies. It reflects the individual enlightenment that happens when this balance is complete on a very deep level. I recently described it in the following way: "The wide-awake witness dissolves into the flow of life and awareness perceives both in nothingness."[5]

Sheldon Nidle also wrote and talked about enlightened society and gave some very useful ideas for creating more enlightened structures here on Earth. I'd say one of the main points was that such a society is mission focussed. In other words those in incarnation support each other in order that each may fulfil the task they incarnated to fulfil. I have jokingly said many times that in a more enlightened society each baby would emerge from its mother's womb waving a copy of its horoscope! The family group would study it and find out the best way to support the newcomer in realizing his or her full potential, and thus complete whatever had been set as a goal for that particular incarnation.

Sheldon Nidle also told about the different stages of development each being would pass through in what he called "Galactic Society". The first "law" to master would be "The Law of One" where each develops his or her potential as an individual. Next would come "The Law of Two" – two individuals learning and developing real relationship and mutual support. Later would come the third and fourth laws to do with relating and working in harmony with an extended family group and then in larger community. All beings would develop in an atmosphere of mutual love,

---

[5] Satsang – may 2000

support and respect. There are many communities on Earth today who attempt to practice such ideas and they are living the blueprints for a more enlightened society in the future.

According to Sheldon Nidle's teachings, Galactic Society also practices "fluid management" where people lead because of the skills they possess when those skills are needed. Hopefully the time will soon arrive when people are supported in order to shine when the time is right and take a back seat when the time is right for that. We will focus on cycles, individual and collective, and people will be free from the stress of having to perform and keep up the façade when what they really need is quiet time for introspection. Such awareness will also help us to recognize when it is a good time for a child to push ahead and learn many new skills or when help is needed to balance emotional energies. The present day examination system completely ignores our deeper inner rhythms.

To finish off this chapter I would like to say that if we look upon Sirius, the Pleiades and other constellations in the heavens through third dimensional eyes we will see people, places and systems. Yet we can also see them as levels of consciousness accessible to us as we lift our consciousness. We can begin to resonate with these levels within ourselves, and Earth will begin to do the same as we open up her vortexes and activate the full potential of her sacred sights. Even though it can be interesting to study advanced technologies and systems of government, it is really important to access the level of consciousness from which these things arise.

The unconditional love that arises from this consciousness is also important for humanity. We have seen that the Sirians do not judge the Anunnaki and simply attempt to help them to feel. There are many of us here on Earth who work in the same way and this can be very provocative for people who are still into judgement and who want someone to blame (or praise). This simply keeps the "us and them" drama going.

It is not really important if all the "facts" I have presented here are exactly right. It doesn't really matter. What does matter is the next step ahead. What matters are pathways that take people to the next level. I offer so much information in this book because many people have forgotten what really matters and want information to satisfy the mind. The singing heart is already satisfied – it already knows the way. So, for the singing heart, here's Monty Python's version of a song (*overleaf*)…

The Galaxy Song

Just remember that you're standing on a planet that's evolving
Revolving at 900 miles an hour
It's orbiting at 90 miles a second so it's reckoned
A Sun that is the source of all our power.
The Sun and you and me and all the stars that we can see
Are moving at a million miles a day
In an outer spiral arm at 40,000 miles an hour
Of the galaxy we call The Milky Way.

Our galaxy itself contains a hundred billion stars
It's a hundred thousand light years side to side.
It bulges in the middle 16,000 light years thick
But out by us it's just 3,000 light years wide.
We're 30,000 light years from Galactic Central Point
We go round every 200 million years
And our galaxy is only one of millions of billions
In this amazing and expanding universe.

The universe itself keeps on expanding and expanding
In all of the directions it can whiz
As fast as it can go the speed of light you know
12 million miles a minute and that's the fastest speed there is.
So remember when you're feeling very small and insecure
How amazingly unlikely is your birth
And pray that there's intelligent life somewhere up in space
'Cos there's bugger all down here on Earth!

12

Bill and Ben the Flowerpot Men (leading humanity up the garden path)

On the 1st of November 1999 I received an email from someone named Daniel. He was responding to a "Bill and Ben" article I had written which had later been published on David Icke's website. The article is included in this chapter.

I'd also like to say that for some reason I had decided to include the Bill and Ben article in this book long before I received Daniel's email. I really didn't know at the time why I was including it – somehow it didn't seem to fit with the rest of the book. I wrote in the chapter heading and downloaded the article, deleted it again and then put it in once more. Not understanding what was going on, I just decided to leave it until a later date and see what happened! Here is the email message from Daniel – just exactly as he wrote it:

> "Jacqueline, I think I can help you with a further "Bill and Ben" connection. In January 1997, there was an interview with David Bowie broadcast on ITV (late night). The interviewer asked him at one point about the connection between the recurrent alien themes of his work and the fashionability of alien motifs then (1997) in the media etc. Bowie, as he has on other occasions deflected the question by saying more-or-less

that he really only uses alien themes as a metaphor. However, at the close of the programme he quoted from Bill and Ben – the line about thinking that the house knows something[1] – as a way of getting across that his answer to that 'alien' question had not been exactly "straight".

"Bowie's cousin is quoted as saying that when David was a child everything stopped for *The Quarttermass Experiment* and *Bill and Ben.*

"To reinforce that this is not an irrelevant link – in the early 1980s, Bowie starred as *Baal* in a major BBC TV production.

"Check out the lyrics of his 1972 song *The Jean Genie.*

"Bye, Daniel."

After receiving this email I did wonder if I should pass it on to David Icke, but as I knew David was very busy and wasn't really sure of the significance of the message I decided to wait. Later that evening I was reading the *Daily Mail* newspaper and came across Jonathon Cainer's Astrology section. Jonathon Cainer is an excellent astrologer and I know from experience that his daily readings are usually very accurate. I am a Libran and what was written for Libra that day really caught my attention. It was something about Librans having a piece of information which they were holding on to because of not wanting to be a nuisance to someone else. It was written that it was

---

[1] I seem to remember that at the end of each episode of Bill And Ben we were told that perhaps the house knew something about what had been happening whilst the gardener was away for lunch

important to pass this information on – important not for one's own sake but for the sake of many others. I then felt I should pass the information on to David Icke.

Not really being a David Bowie fan, I didn't know the song *The Jean Genie* and asked a few people if they knew the words so I could include them in an email to David, but they didn't. Early next day I decided to send the email to him even though I couldn't include the words of the song. I went to turn off the radio before writing the email and just as I almost had my hand on the switch I heard the radio presenter announce David Bowie with *The Jean Genie*! I was stunned. Here are some of the lyrics as I heard them:

> "The Jean Genie lives on his back
> Sits like a man but smiles like a reptile
> He's outrageous he screams and he bawls
> With the Jean Genie let yourself go."

I tuned into the whole happening and asked what I needed to know from this. All that came to me was the word "triggers".[2] I have, as yet, no conclusion to this strange sequence of events. Here is a slightly revised edition of the original Bill and Ben article:

For a few years I occasionally worked together with David Icke and in this way received much very valuable information about the manipulation of consciousness on this

---

[2] It is known that many in the music industry have been used to put out "trigger words" in their songs. These are words that trigger the programming of those who have in some way been subjected to mind control programming. Read *The Music Of Time* by Preston B. Nichols (Sky Books) and *Trance-Formation Of America* by Cathy O'Brien and Mark Phillips (Reality Marketing Inc, Las Vegas, Nevada, USA 1995)

planet. When we worked together David presented this information in his own unique way and I worked with meditation and special energy work designed to connect people to a level beyond that from which the energy used to manipulate consciousness comes from. I feel it is important that people are willing to look at what is happening on the planet – at what I call the collective shadow – and at the same time go deeply into meditation so they do not get lost in what is happening.

One morning I tuned in to receive inspiration for the work I was to do with David in the time ahead. I was surprised to suddenly seem to be watching an old television program many of you may remember, *Bill and Ben the Flowerpot Men*. It was an afternoon program for very young children and was a story about two small men who were flowerpots and their female friend who was a weed. She had a high, squeaky voice and was usually addressed as "Little Weed". Whenever anyone spoke to her the usual reply was a very squeaky "weeeeeeed". Bill and Ben themselves spoke gibberish. What I seem to remember most was something like,

> "Ohhh shlobalobalob", followed by Little Weed's squeaky reply, "Weeeeeed".

The three of them played together in a garden and the story usually ended with the gardener coming back from his lunch break and Bill and Ben disappearing back into their flowerpots. What had this funny little story to do with my work with David Icke in the time ahead? I had no idea.

A couple of weeks later I was doing some work with David in Hebdon Bridge, England. At one point whilst the group participants were being led through a guided imagery exercise, I closed my eyes and suddenly found myself in London looking at buildings. I started out at Big Ben and then saw different views of London, some from the air. I was very much aware of the gold (symbol of the Sun) which had been used on many buildings. Later on, whilst talking to the group, David suddenly mentioned Bill and Ben the flowerpot men. He just made a few comments and jokes about the program and then carried on with his talk. Afterwards I asked David if there was any special reason he'd brought up the subject of Bill and Ben. He said there were none that he was conscious of.

As a supplement to his talk David showed color slides including slides of Bohemia Grove, north of San Francisco, where Satanists still perform human sacrifices to the Sun god Baal – also known as Bel or Bil. Those who take part in Bohemia Grove activities are known as, "Grovers". Several politicians and other well-known public figures that work covertly for the global elite or "Brotherhood" agenda of the New World Order are known to be members. For readers who are not aware of this elite agenda I can briefly say that its goal is a microchipped population under the control of a one world government and one world army. A detailed account of the activities at Bohemia Grove is given in two very good books I have read and can recommend. The first is, *Trance Formation of America* by former White House mind controlled slave Cathy O'Brien, and the man who rescued and deprogrammed her, Mark Philips. The other is a book written by David Icke entitled, *I am Me I am Free*.

I began to sense a connection between Bill, of Bill and Ben, and the sun god Baal. Then I wondered what part Ben had to play. Later that day as the group was being taken through another exercise I closed my eyes for a while and again found myself hovering above the streets of London. This time I was aware of the fact that my face was right in the face of Big Ben. It was almost as if I hadn't quite got the message earlier and now it was, "in my face", as the saying goes! I was to make the connection between Ben and Big Ben. Suddenly it all fell into place. My Bill and Ben "vision" was awakening me to the importance of the Mayan Calendar, which I had only recently begun to look at.

Bill symbolises Bil, Bel or Baal, a Phoenician Sun God. The Sun cult said to be at the roots of the hidden manipulation of this planet is connected with Baal worship. For more information read *The Biggest Secret* by David Icke. Ben symbolizes Big Ben and the mechanization of time – humanity locked into third dimensional time and therefore delinked from spiritual source. The third dimension vibrates at a slower speed than the dimensions above it, and this vibration keeps our consciousness locked into a very limited way of perceiving reality. And what about Little Weed? She's the only female in the program and she's not even a flower, just a weed. For me, she suddenly symbolized the idea of the disempowerment of the feminine. (Remember I'm looking at symbols here – I've nothing against weeds!)

I decided to include in the workshop what I knew about the Mayan Calendar and suddenly many things fell into place for all of us. So here is what I find relevant to share with you in this article. I do recommend people having a Mayan Calendar reading, as it is another way of shedding light on the dharma or mission of a particular incarnation. Remember however that a good reading will simply inspire you to be who you are and to do what feels natural. It is no substitute for living your life, "following your bliss" and just getting on with it! The Sanskrit word "dharma" means doing what comes naturally. To Anton Kornblum in England, who works with the Mayan calendar, I am grateful for the information he has shared with me on this subject. It has inspired much of what now follows.

According to Mayan cosmology, about 5,200 years ago humanity reached a point in its evolution from where it was possible to make a leap in consciousness – a quantum leap – to a new level. In the calendar I work with, the point humanity had reached is the final point on the yellow castle of giving and ripening. The new level, which was possible, is refered to as the green castle of enchantment. The forces controlling the planet saw this imminent lift in consciousness as a threat to their agenda and sabotaged it. So instead of rising, we fell. That's the so-called "bad news". Here comes the "good news". The Mayan calendar comes to an end in December 2012. Some people worry that this may signify the end of the world. (In chapter 5, in connection with Project Bluebeam, I talk about how this fear could be manipulated to create more fear amongst people.) However, in a way, it may signify the end of the world. We could say it signifies the end of the world, as we know it – the end of a world imprisoned in third dimensional space and time. It does not signify the end of life. The world we have created no longer leaves much space for life. When I hear people say that perhaps the world is coming to an end I say, "Good. The sooner the better!"

You see, according to Mayan cosmology, when we reach December 2012 we stand once again at the end of the yellow castle ready to make a leap in consciousness into the green castle of enchantment. This time I feel we are going to make it. Sometimes when I look at what is happening in the world

I'm not sure how we are going to make it! Yet I feel deep inside that we are going to take this planet through the lift in consciousness it has so long been waiting for.

The fact that the Mayan calendar ends at the end of 2012 I also find quite intriguing for another reason. I remember reading somewhere that the future can also affect the now and this is the possibility we see here. We have a possible future – a scenario created by a group of highly evolved beings. This scenario is causing many people to look at where we're heading and to question the significance of 2012. We have many people who are now very focussed on fulfilling their full spiritual potential and who feel they have to make an effort so they are ready for 2012. They are actually contributing to the fulfillment of the positive potential in this prophecy. I found a lovely piece about the Mayan Calendar in *The Pleiadian Agenda*. Here it is:

> "...the calendar is like an etheric aerobics class that gets you to focus on the quality of your ideal body and work towards this ideal day-by-day."

Part of the manipulation of consciousness on this planet works by delinking people from their spiritual source and persuading them that this third dimensional world is all there is. The masculine energy is over emphasized and the feminine suppressed. This is reflected in the Gregorian calendar we use which focuses on the 12 solar months and ignores the 13 moon phases. The Mayan calendar is a perfect balance of the Sun and Moon – the masculine and feminine. The Mayans knew that our planet and solar system are closely linked to Alcyone, the brightest star in the Pleiades. They knew that Alcyone is like a 20 faceted diamond reflecting 20 aspects of the masculine energy to us. These 20 facets are presented as 20 glyphs or symbols. Combined together with the 13 aspects of the Moon, we have 260 possible combinations of energy or days on which to be born, and therefore 260 "galactic signatures" we can be born with. This means that tuning in to the Mayan signature for each day tunes us in to the cosmos and to a perfect balance of masculine and feminine energy.

In the way we measure time on this planet the full significance of the 13 Moon cycle has been ignored. We are even persuaded that the number 13 is unlucky! Let's look at what happens when people incarnate on a planet where the feminine energy is suppressed. First of all we create an energy field where women are disempowered and this we have certainly seen on Planet Earth. There are probably billions of women throughout time who have felt themselves playing, or being expected to play, "Little Weed" roles. Men who incarnate into such an energy field also find it difficult to access their inner feminine energies and we therefore create the "Macho man" ideal which men have been expected to live up to. As the number 13 also represents the higher feminine or spiritual energies, by diminishing it we create an energy field where contact with our spiritual source is forgotten or difficult to access. People come here and forget who they are. They imagine this physical world, physical body and earthly possessions are all there is. We have fear, competition and war as people fight to defend what they think is theirs. These are the very energies that keep us locked into third dimensional space and time and which feed the force manipulating the planet. Let us also not forget that this energy also creates a reality where we see others "out there" manipulating the planet and thus lose contact with the fact that on another level it is simply one flow of consciousness, a divine drama we on Planet Earth participate in. Losing sight of this also perpetuates the illusion and keeps us trapped in it.

Another way we can look at this is to see the number 13 as symbolizing figures like Jesus or King Arthur. Whether or not they existed in the way generally reported is not important here. Jesus is said to have had 12 disciples and King Arthur 12 knights. Remove the number 13, Jesus or King Arthur, and you remove the enlightened consciousness and are left with the disciples or followers. So on Planet Earth we could end up with six billion disciples – perhaps David Icke would call them "disheeples" – and no one who could see the way ahead! As I always say, the only way out for this planet is enlightenment or higher consciousness. This means we need enough people with this kind of consciousness to be able to bring an enlightened energy down onto the physical plane and into the heart of every structure created here.

The manipulation of consciousness on this planet operates from the lower 4th dimension which some call the astral plane. Higher consciousness, sometimes called Christ consciousness, Buddha consciousness or simply enlightenment, brings in an energy from beyond the 4th dimension. It brings with it a consciousness whose realization is oneness, and in this realization separatism and the wish to control and manipulate others cannot exist. This energy dispels the illusion and reconnects us so we again experience the one consciousness pouring through all life forms.

I was aware of the work of José Arguelles already in 1987 when I helped to create and participated in ceremonies in connection with Harmonic Convergence. However it was only in 1997 when I heard José speak at a conference in Arizona that I received an understanding of the Gregorian calendar as a tool for the suppression of consciousness. Lately I have also come to another understanding. It seems the Gregorian calendar may have been manipulated into place so that we got the millennium at the end of what we call 1999. There was an enormous acceleration of Sun spot activity at this time and during the year 2000 and, as we know from research that has been done, an increase in solar activity creates an increase in energy. More energy simply means there is more energy available either for the upliftment of consciousness or for the suppression of consciousness. The more fear, anger and panic created around this point in time, the more the energy could be used to perpetuate the manipulation of consciousness. The more love and joy created, the more we could use the energy for a collective lift in consciousness. Having the millennium when we had it gave us the opportunity for either. Looking at the One World Order agenda I saw the possibility of many cards being played to increase the fear level on the planet. We had Y2K, threats of economic disasters, many fearful prophecies for 1999 and there was even talk of possible extraterrestrial scenarios that could be played out such as holographic technology faking "alien "invasions".

Before I was aware that the Gregorian calendar had most probably been set to allow the possible manipulation of consciousness around the millennium, I was looking at the hidden information that would be coming to the surface in 1999. I was tuning in to what part I had to play in all of this and what came to me was to name 1999 as the Year of Celebration and thus bring awareness to the idea of celebration as a pathway to peace and enlightenment. Many people responded to my invitation to set up celebrations and other events that in some way could give people an understanding of the power of the joy of the heart. One of the main goals of this project was to bring to people's awareness the fact that whatever happened that year they had a choice. They could either close down in fear and negativity or consciously choose to keep the heart open and keep on celebrating life – *no matter what!* This project was really about collective alchemy – looking at what is happening in the world, embracing the facts and yet still keeping the heart open and celebrating life. Just look at what power we have available in the heart. If people choose not to go into fear we can use the energy flooding the planet for a great upliftment of consciousness. Somewhere inside I kept hearing the phrase, "What if they had a war and nobody came!" Then I found myself saying, "What if they staged an alien invasion and nobody went into fear because they knew it was holographic technology!" That would certainly help to stabilize the collective energy fields!

When I first announced I was calling 1999 the Summer of Celebration, some people said they liked the idea but felt I should save it for the year 2000. I was told no one would want to celebrate in 1999, as they'd all be getting ready for the millennium. My reply was that I didn't know why it had to be 1999, but I just knew that was the case. A little later I found out about the significance of the Gregorian calendar and how it had created the millennium shift at this particular time. I then felt I understood why we needed to celebrate and really acknowledge the power of the heart in 1999.

In an article I wrote about this project I talked about dancing for peace and enlightenment, and said I meant this to be taken symbolically and / or literally. A dancing and singing heart cannot be manipulated. I often say that, for me, the word "celebration" really means every cell vibrating with the higher consciousness – Cell – Vibration! I also talk about "collective alchemy". What I mean by this is enough people choosing to turn the base metals of fear, pain, anger, resentment and hatred into "gold". The gold here is the love lying as a potential deep within every heart. I suggest that the path of celebration and collective alchemy be used in the years ahead and up to the year 2012. If you meditate alone or in groups you may wish to help nourish the two seeds I planted in the collective consciousness during an energy celebration I held at an ashram in Denmark in 1998. The seeds are:

> "May all beings recognize the power of the heart as an alchemical tool."

> "May all beings take responsibility for whatever life provokes within them and consciously choose the path of alchemy for the upliftment of consciousness on the planet."

As I see it, the way we move through the time ahead can really make a difference as to whether we have a smooth or rough ride up to the year 2012. Ultimately whichever ride we have will be the one we have and totally OK in that way! There is a fine balance to be found between negativity and positivity. Neither takes us beyond the duality. So we need to accept both possible outcomes and then we can choose to play our parts in the cosmic scripts as beautifully as possible. I hope you enjoy the ride!"

13

Shamballah – inner state or inner Earth?

This is a chapter where I shall be presenting many short stories without promising any definite conclusion, as I do not claim to have the full answer to what is happening inside of this planet. I believe things are happening on many levels. When I present material in this way I sometimes suggest a way of working with it that stimulates the intuition. This technique is given at the end of the chapter and you are welcome to try it.

One evening back in 1995, before I was actually introduced to the subject of the "conspiracy", I was holding an evening of energy work in Copenhagen. Towards the end of the evening I asked people to close their eyes and to allow a geographical spot on the planet or a current political event to present itself. I was simply going to ask each individual to direct a neutral healing energy to the place or situation. I was very surprised to find myself confronted with Antarctica – an area about which I knew next to nothing. I asked inside what this was about and was told there were bases there that I should focus my energy on. This I did but did not have a clear feeling as to what the bases were about or why my energy was needed there.

A few years ago David Icke told about a man who had been flying a plane near the North Pole. The engine suddenly cut out, the plane stopped and then slowly descended into the earth where he was met by very tall, blond haired, beings with bluish lazar-like eyes. They were wearing Maltese Crosses around their necks. I told this story in detail during an evening talk I held somewhere in Scotland and afterwards a woman from the audience came to me with an interesting story. She was an artist and told how, several years earlier, she had suddenly found herself making a ceramic Maltese Cross. She said she seemed to be obsessed by it – a bit like the man making a model of a hill in the movie *Close Encounters of the Third Kind* – and said that she couldn't stop working on it until it was exactly right. She showed me a photograph of it – very beautiful. It actually had an Arabian mosque feel about it. Once finished she didn't quite know what to do with it and hung it outside of the building where she had her studio.

Some time later she was sitting in the studio and the door seemed to open and a group of very tall, blond, blue eyed beings entered. She said that what actually happened seemed to be happening on a physical-etheric level. The beings started to examine everything in the studio as if they were making a thorough search of the place, and as they did this they ignored her. She said she didn't find them threatening and that they seemed totally neutral. After a while, however, she felt it was all "a bit too much" and left the room. When she returned some time later they had gone and, suddenly feeling quite perplexed over what had happened, she told her husband about the visit. He is very intuitive, and his immediate response was that he felt the visit had taken place because of the Maltese Cross she had hung outside of the building.

Some time later, still in Scotland, someone suggested I talk with an Australian who might also have something to tell which would be of interest to me. I met this man and interviewed him and, yes, he did have an interesting story to tell. He had had several extra-terrestrial encounters in Australia but the following account is most relevant to this story. This is what he said:

> "When I was about 17 or 18 years old I had an encounter with a very tall, blond, blue eyed being with a very pointy chin. He gave me a piece of metal, about credit card size, and there were strange patterns on it. It looked a bit like a computer microchip. The being said that this was a passport of my life and contained my past, present and future. I was told that all the information was on it and that I could keep it for 24 hours and then give it back. It was as if he was testing me to see if I could make any sense of it. I gave it to a friend studying at Sydney University and asked if he understood what it was. He passed it around and no one could make any sense of it. He then gave it to someone in the metallurgy department to find out what kind of metal it was. It looked like aluminum. This person tested it in many ways and then said that this particular metal was unknown here on earth. We had a bit of a confrontation because he wanted to keep it – the department wanted to know what it was – and I'd been told to give it back after 24 hours. Anyway after the 24 hours were up the metallurgy department still had the card and then I was told it 'vanished'. I haven't seen it since. There was a Maltese Cross on the card.
>
> "About 18 months later I was lying on my bed one night, but I wasn't asleep. Suddenly it was as if my body was frozen and I couldn't move. Around me were several beings similar to the one I had met that day. They were looking at me as if I was a specimen of some kind. It felt both strange and reassuring. I

felt they could have communicated telepathically with me if they had wished to. Then they 'evaporated'."

This man had had many such encounters – some resembled my own, and I knew his accounts were accurate. He's a very interesting man, quite a genius too, and not the least bit into sensationalism.

In chapter 10 I mentioned the fact that there may be a jewel in the Coronation Crown of Queen Elizabeth that is programmed with the agenda for the manipulation of this planet. It seems the jewel is actually in the form of a Maltese Cross – a symbol used by the Knights of Malta. In *The Biggest Secret* David Icke mentions the Maltese Cross several times and describes how, during the coronation ceremony, the Queen has a scepter and an orb with a Maltese Cross on the top. He also describes the Coronation Crown:

> "The Coronation Crown is set with 12 jewels along with two depictions of the Maltese Cross which was one of the most prominent symbols of the Nazis."[1]

I would like to make a point here – a point I am sure David Icke would also make. Symbols are powerful and attract a lot of energy for whatever purpose they are being used. They are not positive or negative. Just because the Nazis often used a certain symbol doesn't mean we shouldn't use it – on the contrary! I'd say to people who work with healing and ceremony to consciously use such symbols. Use them, bless them and envision them being used only for the highest good. In this way we can reverse the negative energies created around these symbols. The

---

[1] *The Biggest Secret*, chapter 18

swastika, the pentagram and the dove are all examples of symbols that have had their symbolism and sometimes even their form reversed, and have been used to create a powerful energy for malevolent purposes.

I include the Maltese Cross stories here because I do feel that they are connected with at least one group of beings who reside in the inner Earth, are highly evolved and are not working against human beings. For some reason I also feel a strong connection to them. In his book *The Children of Mu*, James Churchward says the Maltese cross is a symbol which comes from Lemuria. Now to other parts of the story.

According to Stewart Swerdlow in *Blue Blood, True Blood*, Reptilians cut off from their home in the Draco constellation, used the inner Earth to plan their takeover of Earth. They planned to blend their genetics with those of the humans living on the surface of the Earth because the Reptilian frequency was already established in the reptilian brain section of hybrid humans. They prefered the genetics of blonde-haired, blue-eyed people and abducted political leaders and members of the ruling classes.

The Hopi Indians have a legend about a lizard like race that occupied an ancient tunnel under present day Los Angeles about 5,000 years ago. Today it is said that the tunnel has been found and that malevolent Freemasonic rituals take place there.[2] There are other stories connecting the reptilians with underground tunnels and bases and there are also many other accounts of inner earth experiences.

I also recommend a book called *The Hollow Earth*[3] written by Dr Raymond Bernard. Amongst other things this book

---

[2] *The Biggest Secret*, chapter 2

[3] *The Hollow Earth* by Dr Raymond Bernard (Fieldcrest Publishing Co, Inc, New York)

contains simple theories and facts that seem to disprove commonly held beliefs about the nature of the center of the Earth. Here are a couple of examples:

> "The belief in the Earth having a fiery center probably arose from the fact that the deeper one penetrates into the Earth, the warmer it gets. But it is a far-fetched assumption to suppose that this increase of temperature continues until the center of the Earth. There is no evidence to support this view. It is more probable that the increase of temperature continues only until we reach the level where volcanic lava and earthquakes originate, probably due to the existence of much radioactive substances there. But after we pass through this layer of maximum heat, there is no reason why it should not get cooler and cooler as we get nearer and nearer to the Earth's center."

I also find what Raymond Bernard has to say about the size and the weight of the Earth interesting. I actually wasn't aware of this fact. He says:

> "The total surface of the Earth is 197 million square miles and its estimated weight is six sextillion tons. If the Earth was a solid sphere, its weight would be much greater. This is one among other scientific evidences of the fact that the Earth has a hollow interior."

The Hollow Earth contains much information about the Arctic and Antarctic expeditions of Admiral Richard E. Byrd that took place in 1947 and 1956 respectively. Byrd's discoveries were kept secret and the US government suppressed the information he gave. He actually penetrated

1,700 miles beyond the North Pole and 2,300 miles beyond the South Pole into territories that were not on the official maps. At the North Pole he discovered a warm climate with green vegetation, forests, lakes and mountains. Before he died he referred to the land he discovered as,

> "... that enchanted continent in the sky, land of everlasting mystery!"

I have also heard from another source that Byrd met the famous giants of the Hollow Earth and that when he left they bade him "Aufwedersen". This may make more sense a little later in the chapter, and there is also more to come about Admiral Byrd that isn't found in some accounts of his expeditions.

At the beginning of his book Bernard speculates as to why so much information has been kept secret about Inner Earth discoveries. He suggests that the US government kept things secret so that other nations would not know of their discoveries. He says that it seems the Soviet Union did not have information about these things or that if they did they also kept their secrets. He presumes that if the Soviet Union did know of these lands they would surely have sent fleets to explore and would have claimed the lands as their own. (The book I have is copyrighted 1964.) He also wrote that he hoped some peace-loving nation like Brazil would make some expeditions and make contact with the advanced civilizations living under the Earth. He imagined this race could save us from nuclear war and help us establish an age of peace here on Earth. I found it interesting to read that a South American archaeologist, Harold Wilkins, suggested that the underground cities that have since been discovered were built to escape the fallout from nuclear war fought by the Atlanteans.

In *Blue Blood, True Blood*, Stewart Swerdlow lists several cave entrances and sub-oceanic entry points to the inner Earth. He says the North and South Poles are the primary entry points and that this is why commercial aircraft are not allowed to fly over these two areas. He claims the official reason – magnetic disturbance – is not true. He also writes:

> "All of these areas are closely guarded by local governments and NWO elite forces. Artificially created entrances exist under the new Denver airport, the Giza Plateau in Egypt, major Air Force complexes around the world, and many of the Temples in India and China. A major Chinese entry point is under the Shensi Pyramid that is out of bounds for everyone in Western China."

In Scandinavia we have legends of "Ultima Thule" – a land of great beauty and wonder far away to the north. It is not Greenland as some have mistakenly presumed. However the references to Ultima Thule fit very well with what Byrd and others saw and experienced at the North Pole. The same book actually has an account of an expedition beyond the North Pole that was made by two Norwegians who were also astonished to find a warm land inside of the Earth. They told of a sun that shone beyond the Earth's surface and a meeting with giants who treated them with great hospitality. It seems these giants belonged to a race of Atlanteans who have resided inside of the Earth since before the time Atlantis sank. I imagine that stories such as *Gulliver'sTravels* are based on knowledge, factual or intuitive, of inner-Earth. Bernard also describes mysterious accounts from encounters with Antarctica. His book is well worth reading.

The Hollow Earth stories appear in the ancient writings of the Chinese, Egyptians, Hindus and other races. The Eskimo legends tell of an opening in the North Pole and of a race living inside of the Earth. They also say their ancestors came from a paradise within the Earth. Dr Raymond Bernard suggests that Santa Claus represents some ancient memory of "a benefactor of humanity" who came from this race and surfaced from the North Pole. He suggests he surfaced on a flying saucer, hence the descriptions of Santa Claus flying through the air on a sled pulled by reindeers. In the very early 1900s several people, including William Reed and Marshall Gardner, wrote books about the Hollow Earth. Today I am actually quite amazed that absolutely nothing was taught about this subject in school or in the higher forms of education I received!

Many have searched for Shamballah including the well-known painter and esotericist, Nicholas Roerich who set out in search of it together with his wife and son. Some explorers have actually marked the entrance to Shamballah on a map – there seem to be several entrances, and it is also suggested that these are simply outposts. There are many theories, which state that some who actually found Shamballah never returned.

Another source we can consult for information on the inner-Earth is Jan van Helsing. This will give us similar information from a slightly different perspective. In his excellent book, *Secret Societies and Their Power in the 20th Century* he gives some of the history of Ultima Thule, which he says was the capital city of Hyperborea. (I mentioned Hyperborea in chapter 11 in connection with Sirius because it is said that Sirian influence on Earth actually began here.) He assumes the Hyperboreans came from the solar system of Aldebaran, the main star in the constellation of Taurus. They were said to be about four meters tall – "giants" – and had blond hair and blue eyes. It is said that when Hyperborea sank, its inhabitants settled under the surface of the Earth in enormous tunnels. This realm under the Earth was called Agharta, which is actually the Buddhist name for the inner world, and its capital was Shamballah. Jan van Helsing adds some information I'd also like to quote here.

> "Here we should mention that Karl Haushofer claimed that Thule was actually Atlantis and – contrary to all other researchers of Tibet and India – he said that the surviving Thule-Atlanteans were separated into two groups, a good one and an evil one. Those who called themselves after their oracle Agharti were the good and settled in the Himalayan region, the evil ones were the Shamballah who wanted to subjugate humanity and they went West. He maintained that the fight between the people of Agharta and Shamballah had been going on for thousands of years and that in the Third Reich the Thule-Gesellschaft as Agartha's representative continued it against the representative of Shamballah, the Freemasons and the Zionists. This perhaps was his mission." [4]

Esotericists refer to Shamballah as "the place where God's will is known". I'd say we could ask which "God" this refers to! Jan van Helsing's book actually gives a very wonderful account of the Inner Earth saga and I thoroughly recommend it.

---
[4] *Secret Societies And Their power In The 20th Century*, page 172

It is said that the head of this inner-Earth region was the king of the world and that his earthly representative was the Dalai Lama. The present day Dalai Lama and certain Tibetan Lamas say that people from Agharta are still alive today. Shamballah actually has many names and perhaps I should list some of them here. The names I know of are: Shamballah, Agharta, Mount Mehru, Thule or Thula, Shangri-La, Belovodia, The Land of the Unchanging Swastika, Paradiso. (Long ago India was actually called "Aradiso".) In this book I'll continue to use the name Shamballah. All of these places were believed to be societies living in harmony with a higher frequency – enlightened societies where there was no illness or old age and where people had incredible powers but no power struggles. They are said to have possessed great wisdom. I suppose this is what would be referred to as a "Galactic Society" in the chapter on Sirius.

I attended a lecture on Shamballah in Copenhagen and it was said that a French man secretly wrote a book on the subject and then regretted it and stopped the book from being distributed. However a printer kept copies of it and published it after the writer's death. In the book it was said that Tibet was built up as a replica of Shamballah. Half of the population were monks and could therefore devote themselves totally to the expansion of consciousness. They had a very high level of knowledge and wisdom.

It is also said that Tibet is no longer in contact with Shamballah and that the spiritual standard has fallen. This seems to be obvious if one watches the Dalai Lama initiating thousands of people at a time at Tibetan ceremonies. I have recently seen videos of such ceremonies including one that took place in Hollywood. The Panchem Lama is said to be

the one who was in charge of communication with
Shamballah in Tibet and it is said that the Panchem Lama
will lead the final battle against "evil". Today he is still very
young. The Chinese say they have found the real Panchem
Lama and have produced a different boy. He is, of course, the
child of someone in the Chinese army. As I write this I
suddenly wonder if some "battle against evil" will be set up,
led by this person. What also comes to me is a feeling that
the real final battle against "evil" could be an initiation in
compassion – an opening of heart and mind that would
reveal that there really is no enemy except in the mind. This
realization collectively would bring an end of the drama of
duality and can probably first take place after humanity has
lived out more of its warlike nature. According to the Tibetan
tradition the final battle will take place around 2026 to 2029.

During a recent trip to Rishikesh in Northern India I
visited a man I know who has a lot of knowledge about
Shamballah. We talked for some time on this subject and I
pass on a little of what he said to supplement and reinforce
certain things I've already written. This is a subject with
much room for speculation and what I write here is
quite brief.

I was told that the Tibetans were the last civilization
known to be in touch with Shamballah, but apparently
about 400 years ago even the Indians had forgotten about it.
A great historian who knew of its existence asked many of
the holy men in Rishikesh, North India, of its whereabouts,
but none of them knew. In Tibet, however, there are many
witnesses. There are three main theories about Shamballah:

1. It's a parallel universe – purely another world. Some say
   you can get there physically and that there is access

through something similar to the Bermuda Triangle where it's possible to cross from one dimension to another.
2. That the access point is man made and an opening is kept so they can have people materialize and de-materialize, going from one world to another. There's a special area north of Lhasa in the Gobi Desert where there are actually milestones marking a forbidden area where Sherbas and other explorers are not allowed to go. The area is a kind of triangle that includes NW Tibet, Mongolia and Russia.
3. Some say Shamballah is related to those living under the Earth and that there are tunnels leading to the inner Earth.

The Tibetans were quite militaristic, like the Chinese and Japanese, and were not loving and tolerant like the Indian people. There was a very autocratic, iron-fist type of rule in Tibet, even though at one point it was the most spiritual place in the world. By the time Nicholas Roerich wrote his very famous book on Shamballah many people had lost respect for the Dalai Lama and it was said that most of the big lamas were living in luxury. The man I spoke with also told me that the Dalai Lama is supposed to be in touch with the invisible king of the world who resides in Shamballah, but there are some who do not believe the present Dalai Lama is the real one. They believe he was a false child and that the real child was taken away somewhere. What comes to me as I write this is that perhaps the real Dalai Lama resides inside of the Earth. I remember someone I spoke with recently said it could be that a real Dalai Lama would have been too much for the world as it is today, and suggested he may have been taken away for his own safety.

I don't have an answer to this. The few times I have seen the Dalai Lama in Denmark I have enjoyed his simplicity and humor but never looked at him as a Self-Realized teacher. I thought it didn't matter – Self-Realization is not a prerequisite for working for world peace! I would support anything and anyone who was truly working for peace on this planet. Yet lately I have wondered about these things. I also wonder why so many people who are supposed to be on the path to Self-Realisation seem to be following the Dalai Lama and are being "initiated" by him.

On a recent television program on the Discovery channel, it was said that the Dalai Lama was actually a title given by Ghengis Khan. It was also said that, long ago, a certain Dalai Lama changed some rules and created the idea of the Bodhisattvas – a line of beings who incarnate out of compassion in order to help with the evolution of consciousness on this planet. According to Buddhist belief it is not good to reincarnate. This made it difficult to propagate the idea of a Dalai Lama who is supposed to reincarnate and be recognized as the leader of the Buddhist religion. I know there are many, myself included, who see the Dalai Lama as a political puppet.

Perhaps I do not need to say more here. I hope those who read this book truly understand that I do not write to create fear and separation, but there are things that need to be looked at and questions that need to be asked and answered. There is so much more openness and such a free flow of information today that things cannot remain hidden much longer. Once the truth comes to the surface we can concentrate on freeing up the consciousness of people on a much larger scale. It is already happening to some extent, but I also feel something much bigger is about to hit the fan and that after this happens far more people will be very clear about the way ahead on this planet.

There has also been speculation about the Tibetan involvement with Hitler and it is known that they were with him in Berlin where they taught him tantric secrets. It is also interesting that during the Second World War many Tibetan monks were found fighting together with the Nazis. The swastika, counter clockwise, was the symbol of Thule. Some have a theory that in the beginning Hitler was basically okay and was perhaps attempting to stop a very negative Zionist agenda. Hitler knew about the "Protocols of Zion"[5] and believed in their authenticity. It is suggested he later became crazy with power but that in the beginning the Third Reich had a very healthy mentality and later had to flee. It is believed many of them escaped to underground colonies. They say that the Tibetans joined forces with Hitler in an attempt to stop the spread of the British Empire which was almost totally Freemasonic.

Perhaps I ought to say something about the fact that I mentioned "Zionism" because this often brings a strong reaction from people. It can be misinterpreted as saying something against the Jewish people and this is just not what I am saying here. Very often people who get close to the truth concerning the manipulation of consciousness on this planet end up being accused of being anti-Semitic because they bring up the subject of Zionism. I have heard David Icke repeat until he is blue in the face that Zionism is not the Jewish people but that it is a political group. Members are not necessarily Jewish. Please remember this

---

[5] The Protocols Of The Learned Elders Of Zion, also referred to as The Illuminati Protocols, were discovered in the 19th century. They give a detailed description of the plans for the manipulation that was carried out in the following century

because this cry of anti-Semitism is a wonderful way of sabotaging the work of those who come close to the truth. It is great that many Jewish people have also had the courage to try to expose what the Jewish people are being used for.

Let us also consider the idea that Truth is not against anyone – it is impersonal. However it certainly ruffles the feathers of anyone wishing to suppress the truth regardless of which costumes they are wearing. By costumes here I mean for example: sex, color, religious indoctrination, nationality, social status. I mean the costumes we wear for a while as we act out our parts on the stage we call life.

I was also told that Shamballah was not what people often imagine it to be and that a certain Shamballah project was sponsored by a pro German / anti Freemasonic movement around the time of the Second World War. There are many reports of groups of people discovering tunnels leading at least 50 meters into the Earth. Such tunnels have been discovered in different parts of the world.

In *The Hollow Earth* Bernard writes about Ray Palmer, editor of a magazine called *Flying Saucers*, who published details of Admiral Byrd's discoveries in the December 1959 edition of the magazine. There is an account of what then happened to this particular issue of the magazine. It "disappeared". The plates were damaged so reprinting was not possible, the shipping receipt was gone, one distributor who had received 750 copies of the magazine was reported missing and the 5000 subscribers did not get that edition of the magazine. Obviously there was something in it that people were not supposed to read about.

Jan van Helsing[6] actually asks a question that gives a different slant to one of Byrd's expeditions. He writes:

---

[6] *Secret Societies And Their Power In The 20th Century*, page 172

"There is the question why in 1947 Admiral E. Byrd led an invasion of the Antarctic, why he had 4,000 soldiers, a man-of-war, a fully equipped aircraft carrier and a functioning supply system at his command if it was a mere expedition? He had been given eight months for the exercise, but they had to stop after eight weeks and high losses of planes undisclosed even today. What had happened?"

He goes on to quote something Byrd later said to the press.

"It is the bitter reality that in the case of a new war one had to expect attacks by planes that could fly from Pole to Pole."

Apparently Byrd also said that beneath the Poles was a civilization that used their very advanced technologies together with the SS. More details of this story can be seen on the video entitled *UFO-Secrets of the Third Reich*.

I have known for a long time that many Indian epic poems and legends such as the Ramayana and the Mahabarata tell the stories of gods in their flying craft and of battles in "the Heavens". These stories take on a different meaning when I look at them in the light of what I write in this book. The Ramayana tells of Rama (Ram is one of the main Hindu personifications of "God") and of how he came from Agharta in a flying vehicle.

I also understand that Tibet and Brazil are the two areas from where it is easiest to come in contact with the inner Earth. There are many underground tunnels in both areas. This also could explain how certain groups of South American Indians suddenly disappeared from the face of the Earth. The Incas are one group who disappeared from the advancing Spaniards and there were also others. I've heard some stories of "mass ascension" of these people, and some years ago I re-experienced a form of ascension from way back in the past that took me deep into the center of the Earth. However I somehow always felt there was a part of the story missing. So perhaps some of these people simply went "underground" as they probably had knowledge of the tunnels and of the more enlightened groups who resided inside the Earth. Perhaps this is also where the expression of "going underground" originated!

In the novel *Inanna Returns*[7] that I mentioned earlier in this book, V.S. Ferguson describes the inner Earth. I quote a passage here that sounds very realistic to me.

> "Tara was of the ancient race of the Snake People, the Nagas, a race that lived on Terra eons before my family. The Snake People came from a different sector of the galaxy, from Altair, to live in the center of Terra."

A little later she goes on to say,

> "The kingdom of the Snake people is vast indeed. There are many cities inside Terra, each resplendent with towers of white alabaster. The air is fresh, regulated by extensive systems powered by energy sources at the poles of Terra. There are gardens and crop fields which abundantly provide for the people. The Snake People have a variety of body types: some are human-like, some are half-snake or reptilian. They can see in the darkness, and they can access a group mind if they so desire, with their telepathic abilities."

---

[7] Pages 110 – 111. In this book "Terra" is the name given to Earth

Just as I was completing the third edition of this book I had a talk with a woman who has had many unusual experiences of a reptilian nature. I will call her Mary. Some of her experiences include people with psychic ability seeing a reptilian entity manifest through her, Mary herself experiencing her physical body turn reptilian, an aggressive urge to scratch her face during such happenings and her right eye streaming with water as this energy manifests. She has also experienced many "coincidences" and strange but symbolic meetings with people since these things began to happen to her. I wish to tell of one such meeting here. At a time when some of these things were happening to her, Mary went into a pub somewhere in England and a man who really looked "out of place" came towards her. He said to her:

> "The energy's coming from under the ground and not from the skies."

Then he turned and left and she didn't see him again.

When I am asked what I understand Shamballah to be, I reply that I believe it to be different things on different levels. There are six main ideas that come to me, all of which can be true simultaneously. They are:

1. That extraterrestrials of a high and of a low vibration and level of consciousness reside there. I believe the battle for Planet Earth has been fought in many physical and non-physical areas – on the third and other dimensions.
2. That it also is the source of much UFO activity.
3. That it has a connection with deeper and more hidden aspects of the Second World War, the spread of a

malevolent agenda for world domination string pulled by an extraterrestrial force which can include reptilians.
4. That some of what people are told about the esoteric nature of Shamballah is used as a smoke screen to hide what I suggest in point three.
5. That there are some very enlightened inner terrestrial societies who can help with Earth's evolution.
6. That it represents a very high state of consciousness.

At the beginning of the chapter I said I would give a suggestion for working with the information presented here. It's a simple technique that can be used in many situations and I hope it is helpful for you. If you wish to try this I suggest you proceed as follows:

> Begin by making a list of the main points presented here – perhaps write 1-line headings, perhaps a short summary of the main ideas. Then you can either record these on a tape, leaving some space between each point or ask someone to read them to you slowly, pausing after each point. Before listening you can lie down, close your eyes and take a little time to relax completely. Call upon your intuition to show you what this story is all about and then visualize a beautiful cup or chalice above your heart. Listen to each bit of information and then allow it to fall into the chalice and blend with all the other bits. When the list is complete ask your intuition what this is all about. Just keep your heart open, watch and listen. Perhaps your intuition speaks to you in pictures or in words. Perhaps you just suddenly know. Remember to respect the way in which your inner wisdom communicates with you.

Finally I'd like to say something similar to what was said at the end of the chapter on Sirius. Let the information presented here stimulate the mind and open it beyond rigid belief systems. Does Shamballah exist or doesn't it? Perhaps it does and perhaps it simply reflects an inner state that will eventually be reached. Let us always remember the consciousness aspect, knowing that if something of a higher vibration pulls us towards it, this is because it is reflecting a deeper aspect of ourselves that is waiting to be accessed and integrated. I heard somewhere it was said that the capital of Shamballah was Kapalla. I find this interesting because Jacob said he came from Kapella in the Galaxy of Andromeda. (I know Andromeda carries a very high frequency and therefore represents a high state of consciousness.) Looking at a map of the heavens I see there is a Capella which seems to be the main star in the constellation of Auriga. An interesting coincidence perhaps. Are they physical places, inner states or both? Let us remember the importance of the inner state and the advice to "Seek first the Kingdom".

Shamballah is also the Isle of Avalon of the King Arthur legends, the Land of Amenti from the Egyptian Book of the Dead, the City of the Seven Kings of Edom or Eden in the Judaic tradition, the Land of the Mysteries of the Celts, El Dorado of the Spanish Conquerors in America and Colchida sought by Jason and the Argonauts in search of the Golden Fleece. The list is long and I would say there is an exoteric and esoteric level to consider. Professor Henrique J. de Souza, President of the Brazilian Theosophical Society wrote an article entitled "Does Shangri-La Exist?" He points to the fact that among all races there exists some sort of tradition concerning a paradise on Earth where people lived lives of great beauty and high ideals. Only those who are pure and innocent can know this sacred land and thus it is connected with central themes of the dreams of childhood. He goes on to say:

> "The road that leads to this Blessed Land, this Invisible World, this Esoteric and Occult Domain, constitutes the central quest and master key of all mystery teachings and systems of initiation in the past, present and future. This magic key is the 'Open Sesame' that unlocks the door to a new and marvelous world."

In the eighties I worked closely with certain groups of esotericists. They had much knowledge on esoteric subjects but with time I noticed that the knowledge seemed to remain as knowledge and was not the inner realization of those I met. The focus was on the outer facts – the words. It is my experience that it is the inner journey – the music – and not the words that take us home. The outer world is also a part of the reality but initiation is a journey deep into the center – to the core of your own inner being. Don't settle for less.

14

Has the contact begun?

Some time ago I read a book written by Phillip H. Krapf, a retired journalist who had worked for 25 years at the *Los Angeles Times*. The book entitled *The Contact has Begun*[1] told the story of his encounter with aliens in 1997.

The story begins with Krapf being beamed up and taken on board a spacecraft by a group of beings called the Verdants. He spends several days there, is treated with great care and hospitality and is told he is one of hundreds of "Ambassadors" and "Deputy Envoys" being prepared for future contacts. He describes the list he was shown as "an abbreviated Who's Who of the World" and says he found it very impressive. I quote:

> "The text was in English, but a majority of the names carried foreign – that is, outside of the United States – addresses. It seemed that every identifiable race and ethnic group was represented. I recognised a few faces, and many more names. And, sure enough, pictured prominently was a key management figure at the *Los Angeles Times* whom I know personally."

The message is that mankind is on the threshold of rebirth and that we are being helped along the way. When the time is right, those who have been prepared will use the

---

[1] Published by Hay House Inc, Karlsbad, CA. A follow up book *The Challenge Of Contact* has also been released and there is a website: **www.TheChallengeofContact.com**

advantage of their prominent positions in society to reveal the training they have been through as Ambassadors and prepare humanity for contact with the Verdants. The first public acknowledgements should start in 2003 and a couple of years later much will be revealed as co-operation begins between the governments of the world and the extraterrestrial guides.

I read this book with great interest and felt pretty sure that Philip H. Krapf had had the experiences he describes. The book does not introduce anything that I would have trouble believing in. I visited Philip a couple of times and enjoyed meeting him. I found him to be a very genuine man – the same feeling I had when I read the book. Discernment is always important in these areas and I am still not sure about what was actually behind the experiences he had, but it would be wonderful if his story was true. Because of certain things I have learned these past couple of years, I would like to use the theme of the book to draw attention to something I have said many times before. Be aware if information you receive contains a teaching that takes you a step closer to dissolving into the love in the heart or deeper into identification with the drama. Be aware if it reinforces feelings of separation and ideas such as goodies and baddies.

Something else comes up as I write this and it hasn't really anything to do with the book I have just mentioned. I remember when Jacob and I made our Danish radio series on interplanetary co-operation there was one message we gave out many times to the listeners. The message was to advise people not to try to call down space ships and ETs as they could not be sure what it was they were calling down. Very often people who want to be taken up in space-ships and see ETs are vibrating on such a level that they attract lower vibrational energies to themselves and would be far better off concentrating on their inner spiritual pathway. The contacts that are meant to be happen when the time is right.

At this moment in time I'd say remember we have incarnated to lift the level of consciousness on this planet. I do feel we will one-day work together openly on the physical plane with beings from higher dimensions, but collectively we need to keep moving forward. As I see it, having higher extraterrestrials working with us here in this dimension will be a reflection of the levels of consciousness humanity will have reached. According to Philip Krapf, the Verdants have postponed their contact indefinitely and the message is that, before we can be allowed into space, we have to move beyond the war and violence that is still so much a part of life on this planet.

This message has come through many ET groups and reminds me of a couple of stories from Credo Mutwa's beautiful book, *Song of the Stars*. Stories in this book also remind us that this kind of contact is not new. The first story takes place a long time ago in a country I once lived in and knew very well – Uganda.

In Uganda there were apparently two war-like tribes, the Baganda and the Lunga. They had been locked in war for over 30 years and one day as the warriors faced each other in battle something very strange happened. A creature, which has been described as a huge yellow jelly-like cloud, appeared out of the sky. Apparently it had one enormous staring eye. It landed between the two armies and as it did so every warrior lost his memory. Each one threw down his weapons, forgetting what they were for. Later the creature broke into two pieces and disintegrated. The two armies never fought again.

The other incident took place in South Africa over a hundred years ago. A baby girl was found and was named Mtashana. As she grew up she performed healing miracles and taught people many things. One day the girl ran to Credo Mutwa's great grandmother and asked her to hide her. She said "they" had come for her at last. She was refering to her people who had come for her but who did not want the other people to see them. The Zulu people were very sad. Mtashana gave all her property away and then dressed herself in her finest ornaments, walked out of the village and simply disappeared. She disappeared in front of two hundred people including explorers and gunrunners. Credo Mutwa can tell many stories of such contacts and I had no reason not to believe what he told us.

It seems that the strategy of the force controlling this planet is to keep people in a state of imbalance so they can not properly respond to and deal with the unfolding crisis. A man who attended one of my talks in San Francisco gave me a very fine little book. This book was written anonymously by a group of people who had studied the manipulation of consciousness for some time. The title of the book is *Handbook for the New Paradigm*. Towards the beginning of the book they write:

> "The conception of this group of separatists is that a chain reaction will happen allowing for chaos to such a degree that their focus can reorganize this chaos into their own matrix."

This cannot happen if enough people are strong, aware and integrated.

I recently heard of a well-known spiritual teacher encouraging people to call down Jesus, Mary, Buddha and other such beings and ask them to rule over a particular country. I was actually told there was a kind of election going on and people could tell the angels for whom they wanted to vote. It sounded a bit like voting in another dimension. If, for example, the majority over England voted for Jesus, he would be a kind of invisible Prime Minister for that area. Everyone to their own I suppose, but I'd prefer to see people realizing their own inner Buddha, Christ etc.

Before focusing too much on the contact "out there" it might be a good idea to make sure the inner contact is in place. Here are a few simple reminders of how to allow this to happen. I say "reminders" because these things are not new for most people who read this book. Many people now know all they need to know but can appreciate a gentle reminder once in a while. So here's one now:

1. Choose love over fear and remember to love yourself if fear arises.

2. Drop judgements but don't be afraid to be discerning.

3. The good old "be here – now". It's the space enlightenment seems to happen in!

4. Balance the masculine and feminine energies in the heart. Gently be aware if you tend to be overly masculine or feminine and choose something you enjoy in order to develop the other pole. It can be physical: learning to perform simple ballet movements or do Tai Chi can be a great experience for a football fanatic! It can be emotional: consciously choosing to quietly feel feelings instead of keeping busy or talking them away. It can be

mental: studying something that activates the left brain if you tend to shy away from intellectual stimulation. Spiritually it can be choosing a meditation technique which stimulates focus and concentration or one which promotes let-go and being.

5. Listen to your deeper self. Take time for yourself and create a space so you can hear your deeper self or inner voice.

6. See if any physical purification is needed in order for you to be able to make a deeper contact with yourself. This could be a change of diet, release of toxins from the body, some deep massage, more rest or some form of exercise.

7. Dare to be who you are and trust that the piece you are fits with the other pieces in the jigsaw puzzle. I was telling a group of people I was working with about an American woman, whose name I don't remember, who reached Self-Realisation. She continued to play the casinos and smoke like a chimney and she died of lung cancer. I also remember hearing that she didn't want to have any disciples, as that was not her way of being. Someone in the group told us how happy she was to hear this story because she had never particularly felt the urge to go out and help people. She wasn't a cold person, but it just wasn't her and she'd sometimes felt a bit guilty about this. We had a good laugh about this in the group and I appreciated her honesty. It is important to be able to trust the flow of life and where it wants to take you. And remember – you are that flow!

8. If you feel you need help be aware of who can help you to the next level of clarity. This is not giving away one's power – this is spiritual maturity. There are many people who are now ready to leave behind the New Age glamour with its vast market of gadgets, psychic channelers and ascended masters. Yes – even ascended masters have to go! Many are ready for a real enlightened teaching and teacher.

When I look at what is happening in many parts of the world today, I do see that the real contact has begun for many people. They have started on the inner journey of discovery and are taking responsibility for realising their full potential. I feel part of the preparation for outer contact has to do with people contacting their inner visions and manifesting them in the outer world. One aspect of the work of Singing Heart in the future is to help people ground their visions in order to build an enlightened society here on Planet Earth.

15

Arunachala

"In the heart, Arunachala,
It is Shiva, it is Shankara,
In the heart, Arunachala,
It is Shiva, it is Ramana
In the heart".

Towards the end of 1999 I kept hearing the words of the above song and seeing an inner image of Arunachala, a small, very sacred mountain in Southern India. I know India very well – it has often felt like my second home – but I didn't really expect to visit again. I certainly didn't expect to visit India at the time of the new millennium, but it was as if Arunachala was calling me. Finally I just had to buy an air ticket to Chennai, formerly Madras, which is just a few hour's taxi ride away from Tiruvannamalai, a town at the foot of Arunachala. I began to tell people I'd be spending New Year's Eve on Arunachala even though I'd never visited the place before and didn't even know if it was possible to go onto the mountain at night. I said people could tune in to me there and that I'd be using the Gayatri mantra. Gayatri is a very powerful and pure mantra, which invokes the enlightened consciousness. It is a prayer for humanity and the whole of creation – a prayer that all may reach full realisation of the one consciousness, which pervades every aspect of creation. This realisation takes us beyond ideas of separation and conflict. Some people asked if they could join me in India so I said they could come in January and I'd hold a meditation retreat for those who were interested.

I travelled alone and arrived at Chennai airport in the early hours of the morning on the 29th December and took a taxi to Tiruvannamalai. Just before we reached the town I saw Arunachala. What a powerful sight it was! I took my dictaphone out of my bag and switched it on in case any words came. All that came was, "This mountain is not in this dimension."

I knew I was looking at something very sacred and special and was deeply touched that Arunachala had called me at this particular point in time. After I'd checked into a guesthouse and had a couple of hours rest there were only about 48 hours left before the new millennium began. I talked with a couple of Indians who said it wasn't possible for me to spend the night on Arunachala, but I knew I was somehow going to be there. For some reason I didn't sleep that night and was quite exhausted the following morning when, sitting in a restaurant in Tiruvannamalai, I met a young Danish couple – Alan and Lotte. We talked and I told them why I had suddenly come to India and shared information about what seemed to be going on around the planet at that particular point in time. Alan and Lotte actually wanted to try to spend New Year's Eve on the top of Arunachala and said it would be fine if I joined them.

So we set off together the next day. Alan and Lotte had neat little backpacks and good walking shoes and I had a cumbersome shoulder bag containing, amongst other things, two litres of drinking water. I didn't know it was possible to get drinking water from a clean spring half way up Arunachala until we actually reached the spot. All I had to put on my feet were the silliest little shoes you could imagine for such a trip – canvas type ballerina shoes!

Still feeling quite exhausted and not being properly equipped, I found the climb a bit of a challenge on one level and yet just an experience to witness on another. Alan and Lotte stopped for short breaks but it was time to move on again when I caught up with them. I was slipping around in my canvas shoes – much to the amusement of a group of children we met halfway up. They seemed to think it would be fun to try to help me and a few of them grabbed my arms and started pulling me in different directions. I managed to shake them off and continued. For the climb up and also down again the next day there was only me and Shiva – the spirit of Arunachala. All I could do was to stay tuned in. This energy had called me – it must surely look after me.

As we were climbing the new millennium broke over New Zealand and I began to chant the Gayatri mantra and tune in to people I'm connected with there. We were obviously meant to be on Arunachala that night and got to the top just as the sun began to set. It would not have been possible to continue after dark. We found a spot and Alan lit a fire for a while. He and Lotte sat together on one side and I found a small space on the other side and settled down to do the energy work I'd come to do. For about 12 hours I chanted the Gayatri – sometimes out loud but most of the time silently. Tuning in to different countries and people I'm connected with, I was awake every second of the night. I had not planned to sleep. As it grew dark and the stars came out it was an extraordinary sight – magical, powerful and awesome. It also became quite cold and this we were not prepared for. I cannot stand the cold, but somehow Arunachala seemed to absorb this experience and allow me to continue with the meditation. Lying flat on my back, I settled into a tiny spot of earth between two stones and suddenly realised I was lying directly under the constellation of Orion. There it was, shining brightly in the heavens, until the mists came down over the mountain in the early hours of the morning.

As I wrote in chapter 4, some races from Orion (not all) have caused much suffering on Planet Earth and it seems some still have as their agenda to take control of Earth. So for a great deal of the time until the mists came down I worked with the energies of Orion. I simply used Arunachala as an enormous heart capable of embracing and transforming whatever was brought to it. Focusing on Orion I breathed in all its so-called "negative" energies – the violence, the wish to dominate and manipulate and any attempt to sabotage planetary awakening. I breathed these energies into the great heart of Arunachala where they could be transformed, and then breathed back the purified transformed energy. This is an old Sufi heart technique that recognises the power of the heart and its potential for transformation. Sometimes I was pulled over to the pyramids of Egypt and sometimes to the Greenwich timeline near London. Wherever I was focussed I continued with the Sufi heart technique, Arunachala and the Gayatri Mantra. It seemed that the whole of the energy work that night was centered on the fact that everything can be transformed in the heart. That is the real power we have and if we are willing to feel life, embrace it and keep our hearts open no matter what, then this power can never be taken away from us.

There's a story I'd like to tell about someone named Susan from Denmark. She was together with a friend, Suchata, in Copenhagen New Year's Eve. The three of us are closely connected and they were meditating, chanting the Gayatri and tuning in to me on Arunachala. Susan told me later that just before midnight she couldn't keep quiet – she felt she had to say to Suchata, "Remember Jacqueline always says that everything can be transformed in the heart."

She was really tuned in to the energy on Arunachala! What she also told me was that halfway through the sentence she heard a television presenter in the next room announce that it was midnight. So she left the old millennium and began the new acknowledging that everything can be transformed in the heart. I'd suggest that those were seeds being planted in the collective consciousness and that one-day they will be the reality of the people of this planet.

Using the heart to embrace and transform the pain, fear and all the other shadows, opens us to the endless sky. It reconnects us with the so-called higher dimensions which, ultimately, are simply aspects of ourselves. It takes us beyond identification with a level of reality where separation, manipulation and suffering manifest. This is the opportunity a confrontation with the collective shadow offers us. It presents us with a challenge to rise beyond anything we imagined possible. It offers an opportunity for men to be the gods they are.

Perhaps not all readers are aware that Arunachala is also the home of the ashram of Sri Ramana Maharshi, one of the greatest and most widely respected Gurus India ever produced. His radical teaching of "Self-Enquiry" which focuses on the question "Who am I?" is followed by many as a direct pathway to Self-Realization. A disciple once asked Ramana Maharshi for a spiritual aircraft to enable seekers to quickly and easily cross over the sea of illusion. Ramana replied:

> "The path of self-enquiry is the aircraft you need. It is direct, fast and easy to use."

When one focuses on the question "Who am I?" all false identities are allowed to present themselves only to be dropped again. The one who is asking knows that who we truly are cannot be described in words and concepts. So each identity that arises is simply dropped again. I often say it is dropped into the vastness of Arunachala until the vast empty sky becomes one's permanent reality.

Arunachala is an aspect of us – so is Nibiru and all of these other places. If I were asked to offer a little guidance at this moment in time I'd say:

> "Experience the reality from where you are at – from what seems to be real and true for you. Don't take life too seriously, but play your part sincerely and let your open heart and open mind guide you into the open sky. We'll all meet there as aspects of the oneness – Sirians, reptiles, human "saints" and human "sinners". There is only one sky to fly in. Enjoy the journey!"

Index

2012 prophecies, 67, 181, 193, 194, 199

Aborigine, 35, 108
Active Side of Infinity, The, 28
Africa, 33, 83, 117 – 121, 174
Agharta, 208, 209, 216
Alcyone, 179, 194
Aldebaren, 29, 208
Alfa Orega, 160
Amazon, 99 – 116
Amenti, 220
Andromeda, 8, 24, 110, 175, 219
And The Truth Shall Set You Free, 5
Antarctica, 200, 205, 207,
Anu, 34
Annunaki, 31, 32, 36, 37, 66, 67, 77, 93, 174, 182, 184
Aquarius, 4, 122, 180, 188
Arctic, 205
Area 51, 75
Arguelles, Jose, 196, 197
Arunachala, 229 – 235
Ascended Masters, 58, 228
Ashtar Command, 78 – 80
Atlantis, Atlanteans, 29, 41, 207
Avalon, 220
Avatar, 63
Ayahuasca, 99 – 116

Baal, Bel, Bil, 191
Babylon, 108
Barber, Anthony, 55
Barnett, Michael, 11 – 14, 131
Bartholomew, 10
Belovodia, 209

Bernhard, Dr Raymond, 204 – 207
Big Ben, 191, 192
Biggest Secret, The, 16, 17, 72, 74, 88, 89, 95, 123
Blair, Tony, 43, 60
Blue, Blood, True Blood, 42, 204, 206
Bodhisattvas, 212
Bohemia Grove, 191
Book Your Church Doesn't Want You To Read, The, 121 – 125
Bowie, David, 187 – 189
Bringers of the Dawn, The, 27, 50, 51, 60
Brotherhood, 6, 191,
Brotherhood of the Snake, 35
Buckley, William F, 93
Buddha, 196, 225 – 6
Byrd, Admiral Richard E, 204 – 6, 215

Campbell, Joseph, 108
Cancer, sign of, 50
Capricorn, sign of, 50
Carter, Jimmy, 126
Castaneda, Carlos, 28
Catchers of Heaven, The, 125, 126
Celts, 220
Chakras, 7, 111, 145, 163
Children of Mu, The, 204
Children of the Matrix, 21, 29, 36, 127
Chitauri, 43, 117, 174
Christ, 196
Christian Broadcasting Network, 127
Churchward, James, 204
Clow, Barbara Hand, 8, 77, 173
Coatlicue, 114

Colchida, 220
Contact Has Begun, The, 222 – 4
Cosmic Serpent, The, 100 – 115
Count of Albany, 93

Dalai Lama, 209 – 212
Denver Airport, 17
Diana, Princess of Wales, 16, 17, 58, 59, 89, 91, 92, 147, 163, 164
DNA, 45, 90, 100, 108, 113 – 116
Dogon Tribe, 172 – 174
Draco, 29
Dulce Base, 17

Egypt, 36, 207, 220
Einstein, Albert, 165
Eisenhower, Dwight, 80
Enki, 32, 34, 35, 38, 108
Enlil, 34 – 35
Eliade, Mircea, 114
Encounter in the Pleiades, 21, 87
Engle til alle Tider, 76
Essene, Virginia, 39

Ferguson VS, 35, 38, 66
Fitzgerald, Christine, 91
Fraser, Ivan, 22, 33, 91
Freemasons, 208
Friis, Jacob Norkov, 24 – 28, 42 – 44, 53 – 57, 71 – 73, 93 – 96, 148, 149 – 151, 161, 163, 164, 219, 223
Fuller, Simon Peter, 129

Galactic Federation, 42
Galactic Society, 183, 184, 209
Gardner, Sir Laurence, 36, 37, 96, 129
Gemini, sign of, 132
Genesis of the Grail Kings, 36, 37, 129
Giants, 206, 207
Great Invocation, The, 81

Greenland, 206
Gregorian Calendar, 194, 197, 198
Greys, 74 – 77
Gulliver's Travels, 206
Guru, 12, 61, 63, 64

Handbook for the New Paradigm, 225
Harner, Michael, 101, 102
Heath, Edward, 54, 55, 162
Hollow Earth, The, 204 – 6, 215
Hopi, 204, 174
Hyperborea, 182, 208

I am me I am Free, 5
Icke, David, 4, 16 – 23, 29, 36, 43 – 45, 49, 50, 53 –55, 72 – 72, 84, 88, 90 – 96, 117, 123, 127, 132, 145, 148, 155, 156, 169, 170, 187 – 192, 196, 200, 203, 214
I Am That, 129
Illuminati, 6, 35, 89, 146
Inanna Returns, 34, 38, 66, 67, 216 –7
Incas, 216

Jehovah, 37
Jesus, 119, 122, 196, 225
Jupiter, 31, 41, 133

Keith, Jim, 20
Kenyatta, Jomo, 155
Ketchwa, 106, 109
King Arthur, 196, 220
Knock – Knock, Who's there?, 5, 131
Kornblum, Anton, 193
Krapf, Phillip H, 222 – 4
Kundalini, 63, 77, 116

Last Waltz, The, 16, 46, 65,
Lemuria, 29, 41, 182, 204
Leo, sign of, 125

Index

Lhasa, 211
Libra, sign of, 125, 188
Lost Book of Enki, The, 30, 33, 108
LSD, 88
Lyra, 29

Maclean, Paul, 46
Maharshi, Ramana, 229, 233 – 4
Maldek, 41
Maltese Cross, 201 – 4
Mantra, 111, 229
Marciniak, Barbara, 27, 50, 51, 60
Marduk, 38, 67
Mars, 31, 41
Mass Control – Engineering Human Consciousness, 20
Mayan Calendar, 67, 181, 192 – 197
Maya, 67, 174
Microchips, Microchipping, 18 – 20, 67, 167
Monast, Serge, 65
Montauk Project, Experiments in Time, 87
Moon, Peter, 21, 87
Mother Goddess, 89
Mutwa, Credo, 32, 43, 44, 100, 117 – 121, 174, 224 – 5
Mystery Schools, 36

Naarby, Jeremy, 100 – 115
NASA, 32, 65
Nazis, 203
Nephilim, 36, 37, 174
Neptune, 133
New World Order (NWO), 191, 197
Nibiru, 31, 34, 38, 77, 143, 174, 234
Nichols, Preston B, 21, 87, 189
Nidle, Sheldon, 39, 68, 178 – 184
Nisargadatta Maharaj, Sri, 129
North Pole, 200, 205 – 7

O'Brien Cathy, 191
Orion, 29, 39, 41, 42, 77, 232
Orwell, George, 23
Osho, 11, 84, 101 – 5, 236

Panchem Lama, 210
Philadelphia Experiment, 87
Phillips, Mark, 191
Photon Belt, 68, 179 – 182
Pisces, sign of, 133
Planet X, 31
Pleiades, 29, 69, 110, 174, 177, 179, 180, 182 – 4, 194
Pleiadian Agenda, The, 8, 77, 78, 173, 180, 194
Pluto, 40, 132, 139 – 141, 144, 158, 159
Prince Bernhard, 154
Prince Charles, 155, 168, 169
Prince Philip, 154
Princess Diana, see Diana, Princess of Wales
Princess Margaret, 159
Project Bluebeam, 65, 67, 193
Protocols of Zion, 213
Puttaparti, 61, 62
Pyramids of Egypt, 30, 176
Python, Monty, 185, 186

Queen Elizabeth, Queen of England, 89, 145, 150, 155 – 9, 164, 167, 168, 171, 203
Queen Mother, 95, 159, 160
Queen Victoria, 153, 154
Quetzalcoatl, 114, 123

Rahasya, 83 – 86
Ram, Rama, Ramayana, 216
R-Complex, 46, 49
Religion, 117 – 137

Reptiles, 1, 6, 16, 24 – 82, 111, 151, 152, 174, 189, 204, 218, 234
Reptilian Agenda, The, 43, 46
Robertson, Pat, 127
Rockefellers, 46, 92
Roerich, Nicholas, 207
Ruby Red Reptile, 42, 57, 58, 148, 149

Sachala, 105
Sagittarius, sign of, 40, 132
Sai Baba, 43, 60 – 64
Sandberg, Nick, 18 – 20
Sandringham, 165, 167
Santa Claus, 207
Santana, Carlos, 137
Satanic rituel, Satanists, 55, 95, 162
Saturn, 132, 139 – 141, 144
Secret Societies And Their Power In The 20th Century, 80, 153, 208
Shamans, 73, 99 – 116
Shamballa, 200, 207 – 11, 214 – 5, 219, 220
Shapeshifting, 83 – 98, 139, 166
Singing Heart, 25, 68, 110, 228, 235, 236
Sirians, Sirius, 29, 68, 69, 77, 110, 149, 151, 168, 172 – 185, 219, 234
Sitchin, Zechariah, 30, 31, 33, 93, 94, 96, 108
South Pole, 205
Steiner, Rudolf, 74, 119, 120
Sumaria, 30 –35, 37, 108
Sun, 123 – 125
Swerdlow, Stewart, 204, 206

Tantra, 84, 85
Tara, 176
Taurus, sign of, 176
Tezcatlipoca, 114
Thoreau, 4
Thule, 206 – 8
Tiamat, 31
Trance-Formation of America, 191
Truth Campaign, 22, 91

UFO-Secrets of the Third Reich, 216
United Nations, 45
Uranus, 4, 158, 159

Vaccinations, 119, 120
van Helsing, Jan, 88, 153, 208, 209
van Tassell, George, 80
Vatican, 126
Verdants, 222 – 4
Virgo, sign of, 125

Wilder, Arizona, 88 –90, 92 – 6, 160, 165
Windsor, House of, (Royal Family), 89, 92, 147, 153 – 171
Wolf, Dr Michael, 125, 126
World Wide Fund for Nature, 154, 155

X-Files, The, 67, 75

You Are Becoming A Galactic Human, 39, 40, 68, 178 – 184

Zionism, Zionists, 208, 213, 214
Zulu, 43, 117, 118

Ashram of the Singing Heart

*Moving gracefully and powerfully
through global transformation.*

Singing Heart was created by Jacqueline Maria Longstaff and one of her visions is Singing Heart Cosmic Airport. Here are a few words from her about this project.

> "Several years ago, in Denmark, I awoke one morning with a vision of what I began to call a 'Cosmic Airport'. I saw a kind of airport containing an arrival lounge, departure lounge and transit lounge. The arrival lounge was actually a place where women could give birth to babies in a very supportive and enlightened atmosphere – what you might call 'conscious birthing'. The departure lounge was for people who were dying – a place where they could be supported in dying a conscious death. The transit lounge was for everyone else in 'transit' through life – meeting the ups and downs of life in a conscious and openhearted way. The whole of the airport was a place of joy and celebration – learning how to keep the heart open and celebrate birth, life and death, no matter what."

Singing Heart hopes to create a sphere of joy or "joyousphere" where conscious birthing, conscious living and conscious dying can be put into practice. In southern India land has just been purchased near Arunachala for Nataraj –

Ashram of the Singing Heart. Flame Foundation, a UK based registered charity, works to support Singing Heart's projects and all donations are gratefully accepted. Here are the details you will need if you wish to make a donation:

The Flame Foundation

Yorkshire Bank PLC
211 Whitham Road
Sheffield
S10.2ST
UK

Charity no: **506 106**
Bank code: **05-08-18**
Account number: **33235074**

All donations will be acknowledged if you include your name and address. Thank you.

"When thousands and thousands of people around the earth are celebrating, singing, dancing, ecstatic, drunk with the divine, there is no possibility of any global suicide. With such festivity and with such laughter, with such sanity and health, with such naturalness and spontaneity, how can there be a war... Only in celebration do we meet the ultimate, the eternal. Only in celebration do we go beyond the circle of birth and death."

OSHO

Visit Singing Heart's website:
www.singingheart.dk